BREATHING SPACES

24 BIKE RIDES WITHIN EASY REACH OF LONDON

PATRICK FIELD

**TWO HEADS
PUBLISHING**

ACKNOWLEDGEMENTS

Many thanks to all the cyclists, especially those from the Cyclists' Touring Club, who generously contributed rides to this book. Special thanks to Geoff Apps for his help with the section on land access, Kev Two for riding some of the rides and Sonic Cycles for frame building and repairs.

The publishers are particularly grateful to Lisa Warburton and Sue Hall at CTC for their expert advice and assistance.

Patrick Field came to London almost twenty years ago and quickly discovered that a bicycle was the best way to get around. The possibilities of using a bike, not just within the city, but also to escape it, were revealed to him when he took part in the first 'London to Brighton' ride in 1976. Embracing cycle-touring with the zeal of a new convert, his subsequent employment as an actor meant opportunities to travel throughout Britain and overseas and plenty of free time to explore the environs of London on a bicycle. He writes a monthly column for *New Cyclist* magazine and has a broad portfolio of other velo-cultural activities including running *The London School of Cycling* and acting as a guide and consultant for the tour company *Bike Expeditions*.

Patrick has been a member of the *London Cycling Campaign* since its inception in 1978.

**TWO HEADS
PUBLISHING**
12-50 Kingsgate Road
Kingston, Surrey.

Copyright ©
Two Heads Publishing
1993.
All Rights Reserved.

Cover design by Kimberley Gundle.

Maps & illustrations by *The Design Shop*, Kingston.

Printed & bound by Caldra House Ltd., Hove, Sussex.

ISBN   1 897850 05 0

CONTENTS

GET ON YOUR BIKE

The Joy of Cycling

Fifteen million people in Britain now enjoy the pleasures of owning and riding a bike. Each year more trips are made by cycle than by train and London underground combined. So it's not surprising that in recent years there have been more cycles sold than new cars - many of which have been the fashionable mountain bike. The enormous potential of the humble cycle has been unleashed, and cycling is at last becoming more of an established, respected and popular part of our everyday lives.

Cycling is an ideal source of cheap, healthy enjoyment. Not only do you get fitter, but you'll improve your health and life expectancy. Regular cyclists typically enjoy a fitness level equivalent to being 10 years younger than the rest of the population. Even occasional cycling will make you feel younger. Cycling at least 20 miles a week reduces the risk of coronary heart disease to less than half that of the non-cyclist. To top it all, it's actually fun!

Cycling is important for leisure, visiting family and friends, getting to work, school, shops and offices. It is an efficient, environmentally sound form of transport that has so much to offer today's society. It has never been so appropriate or fashionable.

The culture of cycling

If you only use your bike for work, school or shopping it is missing its highest calling, for the pedal-cycle is the perfect vehicle for leisure travel. A leisure cyclist travels fast enough to experience a changing landscape but remains exposed to every scent and sound. On a bike you feel the shape of the land and can stop anywhere without fuss. You have time to reflect on what you see and your travels will be rewarded with satisfied fatigue and a healthy appetite for food.

Just as non-cyclists tend to over-estimate the problems of city riding, the cyclist who is used to only short purposeful trips often does not realise how easy and pleasurable it can be to ride longer distances. If you can manage a five mile daily journey in city conditions all the rides in this book are well within your compass. If you are not (yet) a utility cyclist these rides will introduce you to the easy pleasures of bicycle travel.

Cycling at an easy pace does not demand a great deal of athleticism. Speed not distance is what exhausts cyclists. The challenge for the leisure cyclist is not pushing the pedals round but being able to sit comfortably on a bike for the duration of the journey. This ability will improve with practice and fitness. Make sure your bike fits and that you have suitable clothes and shoes and you will be surprised how easy covering distance becomes.

Escape from the city

For the city dweller the spur to travel has often been the desire to reach corners of the World where nature is untouched by population and industry. These places no longer exist. The effects of human activity can be detected from the top of the atmosphere to the bottom of the oceans. The Himalayas are scarred with litter and footpath erosion, Antarctica is still deserted and inhospitable but it is no longer a wilderness it is a reserve with bylaws just like any city park. Philosophically there is no difference between the headwaters of Amazon or the River Lee. Exploring the World is exciting, enlightening and satisfying. Distant lands are glamorous but there is pleasure and knowledge to be found close to home.

South East England is one of the most densely populated parts of Britain but it also has a large percentage of England's remaining Ancient Woodlands. The Chiltern Hills to the North West, the North Downs to the South and the agricultural lands of Essex to the North East are all within easy reach. The curiosities and wonders of three thousand years of human movement and settlement, built on and carved into the landscape, are waiting to be discovered.

The recreational rides in this book can serve many purposes: sightseeing; a chance to practice the skills of cycle touring; to take some gentle exercise; to experience the enjoyment of a day out on two wheels. Ride them socially or solo. Ride them fast or slowly. Ride them start to finish or piecemeal - continuously or with frequent stops. Ride them in the heat of summer or when the snow is on the ground. Ride them because they are there. Ride them.

The lucky ones

People who choose to use a bicycle in London find many advantages. They can cover distance more quickly than daytime travellers using any other kind of transport, while still enjoying almost as much flexibility and convenience as pedestrians. Their journeys are more reliable than any other non-walking trips; traffic jams hardly delay them and they are immune to the overcrowding, technical problems, missing services and industrial action which make using public transport such an anxious business.

The regular cyclist not only gains time when travelling but is taking beneficial exercise in the process. The only exercise regime considered superior for all ages is swimming and you can't, in general, swim to work. Cycling is economical. The capital and running costs of cycle travel can vary a great deal, depending on the sophistication of machine and amount of specialist clothing and accessories chosen, but even the most dedicated spenders will find it very difficult to get anywhere near the costs of any other type of mechanical transport.

Freedom & autonomy

This ability to move at will through the cityscape, to have easy access to all its attractions and avoid so many of its stresses and frustrations gives the cyclist a different perspective on London life. New riders often find that this freedom and autonomy, this changed attitude to the environment, gives them a sense of well being which extends far beyond the obvious advantages of physical fitness, economy and mobility. The cyclist with time to spare can vary their route to take in quiet streets, explore open-spaces or run errands. When he is late he can hurry.

London is mostly flat, has a temperate climate and is still relatively compact. It has the potential for a large increase in cycle traffic. Most personal journeys are short enough to be undertaken conveniently by cycle.

Redesigning the roads to allow motorised and non-motorised users to share them safely would not only encourage cycling but, by evening out motor vehicle speeds, allow other traffic to flow more smoothly. Secure-cycle parking requires very little land. As attempts to maintain the image of the car as a symbol of personal freedom becomes increasingly futile, cycle travel will become as classless and commonplace as it is today in Germany, Switzerland, Scandinavia and the Low Countries. In future all work-places will have cycle-parking and changing facilities and employers will be rewarded with a healthier, more punctual and content work-force.

The Future

There are two opposite visions of the future of South East England, the first, the North American model, is a megalopolis where the city centre declines into crime ridden slums from which all but the poorest citizens have fled, surrounded by a thousand square miles of low density suburban sprawl extending from the Channel to Milton Keynes and from the North Sea to Oxford. The population of Britain is not increasing. This building - the Californification of the Home Counties - would not be to accommodate people but would be in pursuit of the impossible fantasy of mass-mobility via the motor-car.

The second model is European and requires the maintenance of cities and towns as centres for employment, trading and leisure. Concentrating these activities means they can be more easily serviced by Public Transport, and that most journeys remain short enough to be walked or cycled. Urban centres remain attractive places to live and work and the pressure for development in the countryside is reduced. The centre of London retains its vitality. The satellite towns retain their character as individual settlements with easily accessible green space between.

Bikes on Public Transport

The ability to carry cycles on public transport is crucial for both the leisure and commuting cyclist. The CTC, LCC and other like minded organisations have joined forces to lobby this issue so that cyclists don't have to turn to their cars as the only way of getting to a chosen route or destination. Nearly a century of negotiations by the CTC culminated in the free carriage of cycles on British Rail to mark the Queen's Jubilee back in 1977 - a far cry from BR's attitude today.

Network South East runs the trains that serve the countryside around London and have a reasonable record of accommodating passengers who include a bicycle in their luggage. Outside the rush hour it is still fairly easy to travel with a bicycle. This may not continue. Passenger trains no longer carry freight or post and new rolling stock has been designed with very little flexible space for luggage and bicycles.

British Rail is being fragmented into smaller units in preparation for privatisation and it is likely that future policy on carrying bicycles will vary from line to line. Limits on the number of bikes per train, advance booking requirements, charges - even outright bans - which all reduce the convenience of bike/train travel can be expected. The best practice is to ring in advance and check which trains on your chosen line will carry a bike. The last resort for completely hassle-free train travel is a folding bike but they tend to be either expensive or unsuitable for anything but short rides.

British Rail has proved to be susceptible to pressure in the past. Several hasty and foolish bans have been retracted. If you find that the regulations have changed or you have trouble getting your bike on a train, complain in writing to The General Manager of the region concerned and point out that you want to give him your custom and money. Contact the CTC, LCC and the Transport Users Consultative Committee for the London area. They are all actively involved in retaining and improving facilities for bikes on trains.

Roads and the Car

At the moment we are poised between two futures. Almost without exception politicians and planners now pay lip service to the needs of pedestrians and cyclists and the advantages that an increase in pedestrian and cycle traffic would bring. The moral argument has been won, but this does not mean a new era of sustainable transport and land-use policy will automatically dawn. The decision making process and the decision makers are still in the thrall of high-tech solutions. The Department of Transport, though increasingly isolated from the rest of Government, is still committed to a massive programme of road building and widening, turning the North and South Circular roads into another orbital motorway, widening the M25 to 14 lanes and a long list of other road developments and 'improvements'.

At the same time public pressure is increasing against road building and the awful consequences of over-dependence on the motor-car. Those who have opposed the growing motorisation of society - conservationists, residents, pedestrians, public transport operators and users, cyclists - for so long fragmented and marginalised are beginning to take a common stance in support of a common cause.

The road-lobby is still a powerful political lobby in Britain. The AA and the RAC call for improvements to public transport and employ environmental spokespeople. Supermarket chains and giant food companies now sponsor pro-cycling events in search of new consumers. The spread of traffic calming is allowing children to resume playing in the streets an amenity lost to them for thirty years.

The defenders of road building try to characterise its opponents as 'anti-progress' but we are the ones with a working vision of the future with many examples of good practice from Northern Europe to draw upon. It is not even necessary to be anti-car, only to show that no transport system with provision for the private car as its centre piece can ever succeed. When the car becomes a necessity rather than a choice

- as it is for so many of Greater London's miserable travellers - the system is failing. Cars are like chocolate. There is nothing wrong with chocolate, but if you try to subsist on a diet of chocolate your gums will bleed, your teeth will fall out and you will die.

The battle for London and its environs is everywhere. Everyone can do something to advance a humane and sustainable transport future and to stop the irreversible destruction that the planned road programme would entail. If you do nothing else join one of these organisations.

Pro-Cycling organisations

The London Cycling Campaign
LCC is the World's largest pressure group for urban cycling. It has over 6,000 members and its staff - mostly volunteers - organise and lobby at both at City and Borough level. LCC is the umbrella for a wide range of activities; lobbying and campaigning, producing data and reports and undertaking the kind of work that Central and Local Government should really be doing. It represents the interests of cyclists in planning enquiries and has been instrumental in the acceptance by Central Government of the '1,000 miles of safe cycle routes for London'. Membership is inexpensive and includes a subscription to its bimonthly magazine *London Cyclist*.

Cyclists' Touring Club
The CTC exists to translate the huge potential for cyclists into reality. As Britain's largest cycling organisation, it has historically defended and improved the rights and facilities of all cyclists, whatever their age or ability, or whatever type of bike they ride.

The CTC has a wide range of services available to help all cyclists. Amongst these are free legal aid and third party insurance, competitively priced cycle insurance, a free colour magazine, handbook, technical advice and information, mail order shop, access to 200 local CTC groups, plus a range of cycle holidays in the UK and abroad. The CTC also does much lobbying to protect your cycling rights and facilities both on- and off-road.

Although primarily a membership organisation, they do have a certain amount of information available to the general public (please send an S.A.E).

Touring

Hundreds of information sheets on most countries of the world from exotic routes such as the silk road which traverses China, to several versions of the Land's End to John O'Groats, to details of the UK Bridleway network. A network of Local Touring Advisers can help with information on local conditions.

Listings for cycle hire, repairs, holiday companies (UK & overseas), and established links with travel agents and carriers.

Information sheets and advice on a range of topics such as how to take a cycle by air, ferry and rail in the UK and on the continent or cycling in mountainous areas.

Specialist maps and an extensive range of books available from the CTC shop and mail order service.

Annual CTC Cycle Tours holiday brochure with around 80 CTC organised tours worldwide.

The CTC Cyclists'Hospitality Directory - a mutual put-you-up scheme. International listings also available.

Technical

Advice, information and reviews on the latest cycle equipment, selecting a bike, equipping it, cycle maintenance, cycle camping, cycling with children, cycling with disabilities, carrying bikes on cars, folding bikes and more.

Member's Discounts

The CTC has negotiated a range of discounts and special offers for its members from reduced subscriptions to cycle magazines to discounts in cycle shops.

Environmental Transport Association

ETA is modelled on a similar Swiss organisation. It offers the same services to motorists as the AA and the RAC - breakdown insurance, etc. - but unlike them does not contribute to funds of the Road Lobby that campaigns for bigger roads and against speed limits and other restrictions on motor traffic.

Reclaim the Streets Action Network

A group of activists with environmental and transport concerns. Their activities range from non-violent direct action to stop road schemes to imaginative 'street theatre' protests against Carmageddon.

Alarm UK

For more information on anti road-building activities. Formerly 'All London against the Roads Menace' Alarm UK is now an umbrella group and information exchange for the whole country.

Contact addresses for the organisations mentioned above can be found at the back of this book.

Organised rides & cycle culture

The biggest hurdle to cross in taking up cycling as a means of extended travel is psychological. People are used to taking out a contract with a transport operator by buying a ticket or to travelling surrounded by furniture in a private saloon. They are not used to setting out to cross country with only a bicycle and a little hand luggage. One way over this barrier is to join an organised ride. You will be able to get used to pushing the pedals while someone else takes care of the route and if you should have a puncture someone will be there to help you fix it.

Cycling has a huge and varied sub-culture and one of the best ways to improve your skills and confidence in any aspect of cycle riding is to tap into this wealth of experience. The LCC has a varied calendar of social rides. Look for rides in the Diary section of *London Cyclist*. These are usually on Sundays and train assisted. The CTC has a network of District Associations who organise weekend rides plus experienced **Tour** Leaders who organise and lead cycle tours in Britain and abroad.

The BCF and its sister organisation the BMBF are the governing bodies of cycle-racing. They have a long list of affiliated clubs. Many of these organise regular Sunday runs for riders with ambitions for fitness.

These organisations are only the tip of the iceberg as far as cycle-culture is concerned. If you want to find out more look in a current issue of one of the specialist bicycle magazines (at the last count there were 15 but the area is very volatile with new titles popping up every month whilst others close, amalgamate or relaunch with new titles) find them in big newsagents.

Here is a taste of rides organised by the CTC:-

CTC TEA - how about discovering Britain with TEA (Touring Explorer's Award)? This is a CTC award that reaches parts other awards can't.

CTC Birthday Rides - a week of rides to celebrate CTC's foundation. It is a sociable event held in a different venue around the UK each year.

CTC Triennial Veterans Rides - held every three years (the next is due in 1995) on a national basis, for CTC members aged 50 or over.

CTC Fun Rides - the club organises a number of national rides each year eg. CTC Century Challenge Series, Velo-City charity ride.

To find out more about the hundreds of events organised by the CTC and their local groups write to the Publicity Officer at CTC or contact the Touring Department.

Commercial and Charity Rides

There are several commercial operations catering for a growing demand for leisure cycling events. If you want a really painless introduction to distance cycling join one of these mass rides and the party atmosphere will get you rolling effortlessly. Sponsored charity rides became popular in the 1970's and there is now a full programme with London to somewhere running almost every weekend from May to September.

Riders eager for international experience can book an organised tour to almost anywhere. These tours relieve you of the need to plan a route and find accommodation. They carry your luggage, offer breakdown services and provide travelling companions. They are a good introduction for the novice who can discover the joys of cycle touring without any of its worries.

It is beyond the scope of this book to include details of all the organisations offering organised rides and tours. Look through cyclists' magazines to find details of the type of organisation and ride you are interested in.

Bike 1

This organisation symbolises the attractiveness of organised one-day rides for beginners and experienced cyclists alike,

Anna Pond and Simon Shaw created *Bike 1* to combine the pleasure of orgainised cycle touring with the convenience and accessibility of one-day rides. They organise a series of Sunday rides, at least one a month throughout the year, which capture the charm of a particular county in a day. The 1993 County Rides series enabled cyclists to discover thirteen English counties and the season's finale is a Christmas Ride. In 1994 they hope to organise two rides a month during the summer. The programme includes rides in support of SUSTRANS (the cycle route construction charity) and other charities.

One of the most attractive aspects about *Bike 1* events is that each ride has a selection of mileages and riders can start any time from 8.30am onwards - this flexibility enhances the appeal to all types of cyclist. To ensure that the rides are most enjoyable they have a limit of around 250 riders for each County Day Ride. The circular routes begin and end at a community hall or similar venue. All start near a railway station and can be easily reached by road. The attention to detail and provision of amenities is impressive; - thoroughly checked and signposted routes, bike mechanics, emergency hotline and first-aid facilities. Most important of all is the home-made food and music which greets the riders at the end of the ride!

If you want to experience the best that organised one-day rides have to offer contact *Bike 1* for their current programme of County Day Rides and Performance Rides.

Selected Mass Rides

May   Bike to the Future - London to Kent, Friends of the Earth 0582 404490

June   National Bike Week - the national event of the year, co-ordinated by the major cycling organisations, the trade and manufacturers. It encompasses major events such as the York Rally plus the London to Brighton fun ride in aid of charity. Also other events organised by organisations such as LCC, racing clubs and campaign groups. Activities range from fun rides to a national bike-to-work/school day.
London to Brighton (British Heart Foundation) - Bike Events.
CTC York Rally - this free event is an annual entry in any cyclist's diary. In 1992 it attracted 30000 cyclists who participated in day rides, team events, fun races and exhibitions.

July   Dunwich Dynamo - London to Suffolk all night ride - Mosquito bikes 071 226 8841.

Aug   The Great Southern Ride - from Eastbourne. In aid of Sustrans - constructors of off-road bike paths - Bike 1.

Sept   To the Lighthouse - London to Guildford Aids Benefit - London Lighthouse 071 405 2463.

ON & OFF THE ROAD

Timing

No running times have been given for any of the rides in this book. The length of time taken will vary with the fitness and aims of the rider, the weather conditions and how often and for how long you stop. If you are an inexperienced rider don't put yourself under pressure - allow plenty of time. I have a friend who insists that the best part of any cycle ride is the stops and all the routes in this book contain attractions worth lingering over. Some could easily be stretched to several days.

After you have made a few trips you will be better able to judge how long it will take to cover a distance. Be prepared to vary your plans - pause to enjoy the countryside and use the rides as a base to which your own routes can be added. If you are feeling fit and ambitious don't be afraid to extend the ride and prolong a most enjoyable leisure activity - cycling.

Maps

The maps with each route in this book should be sufficient to follow the ride but if you carry an additional map you will be able to make your own detours and if you do get lost you will find it much easier to get back on the track. Maps are good for planning and reviewing your rides. Maps can be as entertaining as books. If you are cycling purposefully from place to place a 1:50,000 sheet Landranger published by Ordnance Survey is too detailed to be much use, a fit cyclist on a good road can ride across one in a couple of hours, but for local exploring trips like those in this book they are ideal, with loads of useful information. If you want to do some local off-road exploring you can use a Pathfinder 1:25,000, also by O.S., for detailed route finding.

Food and Drink

The rides in the book have suggestions for eating and drinking but if you want to save money, or be assured of the quality of your repast and be able to stop where you like, you may choose to carry your own lunch. If you are riding off-road you may not want to go in search of habitation to find refreshment. Cycling is always thirsty work and to avoid dehydrating you should have at least one water bottle. A cage mounted on the frame means you can drink without stopping. Cycling burns calories and if your blood sugar drops you will find progress very difficult indeed. This is called 'the bonk' in cyclists' parlance. Always keep some spare food, dried fruit is compact and gives a high sugar return. It may sound foolish to talk about carrying food and water in an area as densely populated as South East England but in the

countryside out of hours you may have to go quite a long way to find a
shop open and then it may not stock anything much except sweeties
and sugar-water, which will give you a sudden burst of energy but then
leave you feeling even hungrier.

What to take

Essentials to carry on a day tour in the Home Counties.

Waterproof and warm clothing. If you are wearing them do you have
space to store them if the sun shines?

Spare inner-tube(s) and a puncture repair kit.

Tyre Levers.

Tools to remove wheels if they are not quick release.

Pump.

Water-resistant sun-block.

Lip-salve.

Food.

Drink.

Money.

Map.

Small tool kit, eg adjustable spanner and allen keys.

Small first-aid kit.

If you are riding in a group not everyone needs all this but check you
have a tube and pump to fit all the wheels.

Navigation and exploring

Finding your way around is not just a matter of map reading, you will
also develop a feel for the landscape. Road signposting is aimed at the
motorised traveller. It sends cars on long detours and often bypasses
the most interesting places, high streets and village centres. On a bike
you should be looking for the old patterns of roads and tracks in use
before the country was bull-dozed for speed. Street names can give
clues. 'Lanes' are usually old routes as are roads named after their
destinations. It is sometimes pleasant to put the map away and just get
lost, it can be the best way to build up a detailed knowledge of an area.
This kind of approach can lead you to dead ends. Old routes can be cut
by 18th century canals, 19th century railways or 20th century
motorways but you might discover useful short cuts and interesting,
hidden places. Carry a map with you in case you get completely stuck
and highlight your route on it before setting off.

Training

Responsibility for cycle training for children lies with Local Authorities, the Police and schools. Shortage of money and unwillingness to grapple with the political issues surrounding road safety, has meant that in many city areas it is unavailable. Some Local Authorities also organise training for adults but these are even rarer.

The LCC operates a 'Bikemate' scheme which pairs novice riders with experienced volunteers who help them get started on the road. The London School Of Cycling offers courses in all levels of cycle riding, including absolute beginners, and also classes in basic and advanced maintenance and wheel-building. Moto Sport in Surrey offer cycling tutorials in on and off-road riding. Several local groups of the LCC run drop-in workshops and classes in bike maintenance. Look in the current issue of the LCC magazine 'London Cyclist' for details.

The CTC are currently setting up a major National Award Scheme with other cycling organisations. This scheme will help cyclists of all ages to gain essential skills such as road sense, cycle maintenance and map reading.

Children

Parents of small children do not need to miss out on the pleasures of leisure cycling. Once a child's neck is strong enough to support its head (around 9 months) it is ready for a seat. This can be behind the rider or in front. For children below three years a safety harness is essential to keep them upright when they fall asleep. If you get a second-hand seat made of strip metal you can use the type of reins designed for use in a pram. Good foot rests help older children spread their load when the bike goes over bumps. Make sure that there is no chance of toes or fingers getting into spokes. Most models come with masking or foot straps to prevent this.

Children have softer skulls than adults and however you carry them a helmet is a good idea. Go for the largest size you can pad out to fit, to leave room for growth. In a childseat the passenger does not have the warming effect of exercise so lots of clothes are necessary with special attention to face hands and feet. This is particularly true of front seats where they are right in the wind.

The further any load is from the steering column the more it effects the handling so mechanically a seat above the cross bar is better. Rear seats whose mountings join the frame near the back axle transmit the shocks of kerbs and potholes direct to the passenger and put a lot of stress on the rear wheel. With the passenger weight between the two wheels the load is distributed more evenly, better for passenger and machine. Front mounted seats have the added advantage that the passenger can see where she is going without leaning from side to side, and that her head is close to the rider for easy conversation in wind or traffic. One type of front mounting child seat is a small saddle that clamps on the top-tube with equally simple foot rests on the down tube. They work very well for children old enough to hang on to the handlebars (2.5 years and up) and are cheap. Bucket seats which mount on the top-tube are available for younger children.

At around 4 or 5 years even the most devoted parent finds it is time to ask the little darling to earn their ride and join in the pedalling. Away from motor-traffic they can ride their own bikes but for roads the best alternatives are tandems and trailers with pedals where the child can pedal while the adult deals with the traffic. Tandems can be adapted with 'kiddy cranks' which bring the pedals up for little legs and later crank shorteners. With a little ingenuity it is possible to use the same tandem to carry a child from around four years until they are old enough to ride a solo on the road, and a younger child can still be carried on a seat at the back. If you are thinking of buying a tandem join the Tandem Club, their members only magazine has lots of secondhand bikes, trailers and family cycling kit for sale. The club is also a good source of technical advice.

If you don't have room for a Tandem or can't afford one or feel intimidated by the mechanical tinkering which setting one up always involves, consider a pedal driven trailer. These excellent machines, popular in cycling's golden years, are making a comeback. They consist of a special rack onto which fits a specially constructed bike minus front forks and wheel. The child has their own set of pedals and can push as little or as much as they like.

On the road

Take it easy
On your first rides out be conservative in your planning, allow plenty of time for stops and exploring. Start gently. If you make an effort to go slowly in the first hour you will find you can go further with less fatigue. In particular keep an eye on the wind direction and strength. Most cyclists have at some time covered a distance quickly, feeling fit only to turn onto their homeward leg and find that the reason for their

zip was a strong tail-wind. An unfavourable wind is the most demoralising obstacle a cyclist can face, on windy days try to plan to fight the head-wind first and then get an assisted ride home. The faster you travel the more troublesome the wind will be so if your route is mixed on and off-road, or flat and hilly try and plan to be facing the wind on the slower sections and have it behind you when you are on the faster parts.

Gearing

On flat roads select a gear on your bicycle which allows you to spin the pedals at least 60 revolutions a minute. It is a mistake to think that unless you are straining to get the pedals round you are not getting anywhere. Cyclists divide into pedallers and pushers but 60 rpm (this number is also known as cadence) is a minimum for easy travel and a rhythm nearer to 80 or 100 is not excessive.

Pushing the pedals too hard and slowly strains your knees and builds up big leg muscles which are useless for anything else except speed-skating and weight-lifting. Spinning fast against a low gear feels unnatural at first but it will help you cover distance without undue fatigue and give you slender and shapely legs. Using a low gear in traffic means you can accelerate more easily and if you are forced to slow down unexpectedly you will not stall. Toe clips and cycling shoes are a great aid to smooth pedalling.

Traffic

To share the road with motor traffic you need to develop two parallel strengths; bike handling skills and the ability to communicate with other road-users, understand and predict what they are going to do and make sure they are aware of your intentions. These skills are no use however, without the confidence that you are entitled to use the roads on an equal basis with less efficient traffic. That you are not only a cyclist but cycle-traffic. Take up your position on the road with confidence and authority, but be aware of the traffic around you and what it is doing.

The level of skill and confidence required to use by-roads on a Sunday morning is not the same as that required to traverse big roundabouts in the rush-hour. Be prepared to progress slowly. Watch how other cyclists manage. You can learn from observing both the skilled and the incompetent.

Bike handling skills

Sharing the road with motor-traffic requires a safe bicycle which will stop and travel predictably. It is a good idea to check your bike over - brakes, tyres, chains, gears - before setting off (see Maintaining Your Bike for more details.) You also need to be confident of your ability to ride it. Before you go on any road you should be able to ride with one-hand on the bars in order to give signals, and to look over either shoulder to see what is going on behind you. You should have a clear idea of how much distance you need to stop in all conditions and how quickly you can accelerate and turn corners. You should be able to cope with uneven road surfaces which, in these days of municipal poverty, can appear anywhere. These skills will allow you to ride confidently with a margin for errors - your own and other peoples. Going on to the road before you are confident of your bike handling skills may leave you frightened, demoralised or worse, so practice these skills away from motor-traffic first.

Once you have covered these basics start by riding on quiet local roads and be prepared to walk any difficult junctions. Sunday mornings or very early on Summer weekdays are a good time to begin.

Positioning

It is a mistake to keep too far to the left when cycling on the road. You should take a line far enough from the kerb to be safe from pedestrians who listen but don't look when stepping off the kerb. When the left side of the road is occupied with parked cars ride far enough from them to be safe from carelessly opened doors. Aim to catch the driver's eye in the wing mirror. The very edge of the carriageway is where you will find the most drains, potholes and other debris so avoid riding here where possible. Traffic approaching from the rear will see you more readily if you are riding where they expect vehicles to be. Vehicles emerging from side roads will see you sooner and you will see them earlier if you keep at least a metre from the kerb. As you approach junctions your position on the road can reinforce your signals to let other road users know where you are going. In slow moving congested traffic take the middle of your lane of the carriageway. This stops motor vehicles overtaking you and blocking the road.

The rules of the road

On a bicycle in Britain you are subject to the same rules of the road as other vehicles. You must among other things show lights at night, observe traffic signals, 'Give Way' signs and one-way streets. It is an offence to cycle on the road while drunk or drugged. You should give way to pedestrians on Zebra crossings and when turning corners. You must not ride on a footpath beside a road. If you are unsure of these check a copy of the Highway Code (HMSO). Parts of the code do not have the force of law but it does contain the guide lines by which road users are expected to operate and may be used to apportion blame in the event of an accident.

Breaking the Code is not criminal but may render you criminally liable, a subtle point which means in practice that many of the rules are ignored. This does not mean that traffic behaves in a random fashion, only that the rules it operates by are not those in any book. In order to ride safely on the road you need to study how things happen not just how they are supposed to happen. Cyclists are often singled out for ignoring the code but it is sometimes the case that cyclists apparently behaving badly are in fact maximising their safety in an environment designed with no consideration for their needs. (J McClintock - The Bicycle and City Traffic, Bellhaven Press 1993).

Confidence

Once you start to ride on the road you realise that road-space in many parts of South East England is a scarce resource and unlike other resources it is not rationed by price only by queuing and congestion. This has lead to a culture of ill-mannered, petty and selfish behaviour on the roads. On a bicycle your need for space is smaller than most other road users but many people in charge of heavier vehicles will still try and bully you out of it. You will often find vehicles creeping across the 'Give Way' lines of side roads trying to make you brake and others trying to force their way past you even when the road ahead is clearly obstructed. Remember that all motor vehicles have brakes even if their drivers try to make you think otherwise.

SIDSY

Whilst holding your ground against the motorists who without thinking are trying to squeeze you off the road, you must also be watching for the one who is not 'bike aware', the SIDSY ('sorry mate I didn't see you'). Look in the faces of drivers emerging from side roads. Assume you have not been noticed until given evidence to the contrary. Be prepared to shout 'Oi' or 'No' at the dozy ones. If they perceive you as pushy or paranoid, so what. At least they see you. You must learn to ride as if you are invisible.

Conflict

Cycling in traffic makes people angry for two reasons, first because they take the injustice of the present transport system -which gives prime consideration to the most wasteful and inefficient modes of travel - personally, and second because it is only by getting furious that they can summon up the psychic energy - the two ton ego - required to make safe progress on busy roads. Just as on a bike you can cut through the frustrations of traffic congestion, you must also make a conscious effort to rise above the bad temper that the current transport regime engenders. Don't be shaken out of your right-of-way when you have priority but don't let the pathetic victims of motor-culture drag you down to their level.

Night riding

Some of the finest conditions for cycling can be found on summer days between dawn and breakfast. The roads are empty and it is the best time to spot wild birds and mammals. Riding all night can turn the most familiar routes into an adventure. Carry plenty of warm clothes and food and stick to roads and tracks you know well. If you are riding on roads it is best to delay your departure until after midnight when the bulk of the erratic late-night traffic has got home. If you use battery lights carry spare batteries and bulbs.

Off Road riding

Bikes

It is not necessary to have a mountain bike to ride off-road. Even lightweight road-bikes can be ridden away from tarmac if they are fitted with tyres deep enough to avoid compression punctures (28x35mm depending on your body weight and riding style). You will have to walk more than on a mountain bike and the wheels will be more likely to jam with mud. A light bike is easier to lift and as many rides will involve a mix of on-and off-road you will save energy when you are on the tarmac. The kind of bike you use will be influenced by your riding preferences but don't let its specification restrict your freedom to explore.

Access

There are four classes of Public Right of Way which are not highways. Footpaths on which cycling is not allowed. Bridleways, Roads Used as Public Paths (RUPPS) and By Ways Open to All Traffic (BOATS) on which cyclist are allowed to ride. On bridleways a cyclist must give way to pedestrian and equine (horse) traffic. In South East England RUPPS and BOATS are quite rare.

In practice the situation is not quite as simple as that. The right to cycle on a bridleway was conceded as part of the 1968 Countryside Act. It is statutory, not common law and can be restricted by local bye-laws. If you see a bridleway marked on a map it is possible that it has a no cycling sign when you get there but this is rare. The CTC, throughout its hundred year plus history (Established in 1878 when there were no roads!), has been instrumental in the negotiation and securing of land access for cyclists. It was the CTC's action in 1968 that ensured the Countryside Act gave cyclists specific authority to ride on bridleways. Pressure is mounting at present to limit such access, so as the only prescribed cycling organisation to receive notification of changes to Rights of Way, the CTC is able to act on behalf of cyclists to prevent these rights from being eroded.

Many paths which see quite heavy flows of cycle traffic are legally classed as footpaths where cycling is prohibited. Even if you see a path scored with tyre tracks do not assume you have the right to ride along it. When you are unsure of the status of a path, but consider it is safe to ride, the best thing is to ride with complete respect for pedestrian or horse-riding traffic. Which you should be doing anyway. Often a short walk on a footpath will connect stretches of pleasant safe and legal riding, in this case the problem is getting your bike over stiles or up steps.

A further complication is that not all rights of way are public. Some are private, and open to only certain identified members of the public - to legally cycle on the tow-paths of canals for example it is currently necessary to obtain a permit from the Waterways Board. In practice, on many stretches, this has not been enforced for many years and almost all tow-path cyclists have no permit and most permit holders have never been asked to show them. In recognition of this British Waterways plan to remove the permit system.

No cyclist should intimidate pedestrians, particularly the elderly, young children or those in charge of young children. If they choose to ride on pedestrian paths riders should not speed and always be prepared to give courteous warnings of their presence. If you find your off-road route congested with pedestrians get off and walk or find a bypass.

An Ordnance Survey Map will have all the public rights of way marked and is a fairly reliable source of information. Other paths or tracks marked do not indicate a public right of way, and may be private. For accurate information on public rights of way in an area you should consult the local definitive map, which is usually available for you to look at if you contact the Rights of Way Officer for the local authority. The larger scale, and therefore much more detailed, maps produced by the Ordnance Survey is the Pathfinder series.

The CCEN (Cyclists' Countryside and Environment Network) was set up three years ago to liaise and co-operate with bodies concerned with access rights. They are active in maintaining and expanding cyclists' rights on routes in our National Parks, forests, canal tow paths, disused railways and other suitable tracks. If you are interested in keeping hard won access open to cyclists and would like to become a part of this network, contact the CTC for more details.

Swamps and other obstacles
Often the right to use a path is academic. Anyone who has attempted to use poorly drained bridleways in the winter knows that it is often impossible, due to damage done by horses or agricultural vehicles.

If you find a Public Right of Way blocked you are allowed to bypass it so long as you do not go onto another property, and leave the land on which the obstacle occurred. You may remove it using tools you have to hand, a pen knife for example, but it is unwise to do anything that may be unlawful. You are not allowed to intentionally use a Public Right of Way to gain access to an obstacle you intend to clear away. It would be unlawful should you find your way blocked by a fallen tree, to return with a chainsaw.

This kind of thing is best left to the landowner, who should clear the way within a reasonable time. You can find out who owns the land by writing to the Parish Council or contacting the County Highways Department and speaking to the Rights of Way Officer. Local Authorities are technically responsible for keeping tracks in good condition. You can also take the matter up with your local CTC and British Mountain Bike Federation Access Officer, These volunteers exist in almost all counties and are cultivating good links with Local Authorities and Landowners. If you ride off-road regularly it is worth making contact with your local Access Officer to offer support and information.

Skills - Climbing

Unmade tracks can be much steeper than metalled roads. Although you can always walk up or down part of the fun can be keeping going on two wheels even on hard terrain. On steep tarmac hills you can stand on the pedals and use your body weight to get them round. On an unsurfaced track this may not be possible because as you lift your body to deliver power through the pedals the back wheel may loose traction and spin. On loose ground use a gear low enough to allow you to stay seated. A low gear delivers power more smoothly reducing the tendency for wheel spin. If the track is wide enough you can zig-zag to reduce the gradient. When the ground gets so steep that the front wheel begins to lift off the ground you have to shift your weight forward over the pedals to keep it down. Then you have to get off and walk.

Descending

With confidence it is possible to descend slopes which appear almost vertical from above. Straighten your arms and flatten your back to push your weight out behind the seat and use the back brake to control your speed, use the front brake sparingly and with extreme caution. Try not to lock the back wheel. You will not be able to steer very much so look well ahead and try to pick a straight line from top to bottom of steep sections. Mountain bikes have quick release seat-post bolts. Some riders like to lower their seats by 30-50mm for tricky off-road riding. This helps them to get their weight out over the back wheel when descending and reduces the risk of injury in a fall.

Mud puddles and fords

Engage a low gear, ride slowly to minimise splash and wheel spin, pedal fast to keep moving (or not).

Hard bumpy tracks

Sit on the back of the saddle to keep the back wheel from jumping around. Lean forward to allow the upper body to pivot at the hip. Support your upper body with your back. Do not grip the handlebars too tightly as this will transmit the vibrations to your upper body. Rest your hands on the bars like a pianist's hands on the keys and allow the front wheel to choose its own track through the bumps.

Tyre Pressure

You can improve the traction of your rear wheel by running it with as little air as possible. This puts more rubber on the ground to give a better grip. You need a minimum of air in your tyres otherwise when you hit a bump you will get a 'snake bite' compression puncture when the tube is pinched between the wheel rim and the ground. If you do a lot of riding on soft ground look for tyres with thick sidewalls which will run at low pressure with less puncture risk.

Walking and carrying

On steep ground, going up, use your bike as a 'Zimmer Frame' roll it ahead pull the brakes on and pull yourself up. Use the back brake to control the bike when walking down steep hills.

It is necessary to be able to carry your bike, not just to lift it over obstacles but also because when mud jams the wheels you will not be able to wheel it. The best way to do this (if you have a crossbar) is by standing on the left of the bike - opposite the chain - crouch and put your right arm through the frame. Swing your right arm round the front of the frame and grab the left side of the handlebars. Stand up with the top-tube resting on your shoulder. Your right arm keeps the bike still while the left is free for climbing. Try not to stoop forward as this will stop you from breathing fully. Stand up straight and keep the weight of the bike well back.

A bottle cage inside the frame makes this difficult so if you are going to do a lot of carrying carry your bottle in your jersey pocket or mounted behind the seat. Don't put it in a bag unless you are sure it is leak-proof. You can make carrying your bike easier by padding the frame. You can buy small triangular bags which do this or tape on pipe insulation which can be bought from a builders merchant.

Erosion

The use of any unsurfaced track leads to some erosion, whether by foot, horse, bike, tractor or other motor vehicle. There is no scientific evidence to suggest bicycles are particularly destructive. The Sierra Club in the USA was unable to establish any clear cut evidence that bicycle riding caused any more erosion or damage than other outdoor pursuits. Even so you should avoid doing anything to damage vegetation or soil-structure.

Try not to spin your wheels going uphill or skid going downhill. Ruts on sloping ground collect running water and become erosion channels. Running your tyres with minimum pressure not only helps avoid skids it also spreads your weight so the ruts you make in soft ground will be shallower.

OFF-ROAD CYCLING CODE

Rights of Way

- Bridleways - open to cyclists. Note that local By-Laws may prohibit cycling but these should be clearly sign-posted. Give way to walkers and horseriders.

- Byways - unsurfaced tracks open to cyclists, but give way to walkers, horseriders, and vehicles which also have right of access.

- Designated Cycle Paths - such as disused railway lines, Forestry Commission tracks, and urban routes, waymarked with a sign showing a bicycle symbol. Cycling Prohibited signs are a bicycle symbol on a white background with a red border. Remain on the designated path.

- Towpaths - British Waterways permit is currently required for cycling on towpaths but this is under review.

No Access

- Pavements - cycling is not permitted.
- Public Footpaths - no right to cycle exists.
- Open Land - no right of access unless on a designated cycle path or with the permission of the landowner.

The Country Code

- Respect and protect wildlife, plants, trees and the environment.
- Keep your dogs under control.
- Use gates (fasten behind you) and stiles to cross fences, hedges and walls.
- Never stray from rights of way across farmland.
- Take litter home and help prevent fires.
- Make no unnecessary noise.

You & Your Bike

- Check it before setting off.

- Prepare your route and take a map.

- Do not bunch - respect other users of the countryside.

- Prevent erosion.

- Ride safely and responsibly - take extra care in the wet and retain control downhill.

- Take food & drink, a tool kit, waterproofs, warm clothes and a first aid kit.

- Always tell someone where you are going and when you expect to return.

- Consider wearing a helmet when riding off-road.

- Behave responsibly - do nothing to erode hard-won access rights.

- Contact your local CTC or BMBF Access Officer or local council Rights of Way Officer if in doubt about access or if you experience problems with access.

BUYING A BIKE.

You & your bike.

Of all machines the bicycle is the most likely to fulfil the advertising cliché, of a possession that expresses its owners personality. The quality of the relationship between pedal-cycle and rider can make selecting one a complex process but even if you know nothing about bikes you can still begin by thinking about yourself and your cycling ambitions. Are you sporty? Will you be riding mainly on roads? Do you want to cycle off-road? Do you want a bike that will take sometime to get comfortable with but has high performance potential or one you can ride easily from day one e.g. a bike that demands special clothes and shoes or one that you can ride wearing your ordinary garb? Do you enjoy fiddling with machines, keeping them clean and well maintained or do you want a cycle you can ride with little maintenance? Will you need to park the bike in areas with a high risk of theft? How much can you spend? How much do you want to spend?

If you are planning to buy a bike for the first time, or are returning to cycling after a long break, don't be put off by the sophistication and range of machines offered for sale. Though the consumerist element of cycling is fun and (relatively) inexpensive, cycling is NOT a consumerist activity. Where you go, whom you go with, what you see and hear on the way is far more important than the bike you are riding. So long as it is the right size and mechanically sound almost any bike will do to get you started.

Don't be too optimistic. It is a common mistake to buy a bike for the kind of cycling you want to do not the kind of riding you will actually do. If you get something basic you can always change its components, replace or supplement it with a more sophisticated mount as your riding style and ambitions evolve.

Bike Shops.

The easiest and safest way to buy a bike is from a cycle-shop. Visit the local shop(s), how do they treat you? Are they willing to listen as well as talk. Do they see you as an individual as well as a potential till filler? Will they sell you what you need or just what gives them the best profit margin?

A shop should be willing to let you test ride a bike before you buy it. To organise a test run, try to visit when the shop is not busy and take positive identification - something with your photograph on it. When

comparing different bikes remember to ask what accessories -
mudguards, toe-clips, lights etc. are included in the price.

New bikes.

A new bike will 'run in' during the first few weeks of use as cables
stretch and settle and bearings wear in. Any good shop will offer a free
first service. Ask what this entails, will they check the spoke tension as
well as the operation of the brakes and gears? If you are not (yet) skilled
in the basics of bike maintenance, you are putting yourselves in their
hands by buying a bike. If you aren't a regular customer of the shop try
and find someone who is and ask them if the repair service is prompt
and reliable. It is well worth spending a few extra pounds to get the
support (repairs and advice) of a friendly and reliable shop.

Even if you are planning to buy secondhand consider a trip to a bike
shop to get an idea what is available and what things cost. This may
sound a bit cheeky but you'll probably soon be back there spending
money on accessories.

Buying secondhand.

Secondhand bikes are often good value but in the London area demand
is greater than supply so you will have to spend some time searching.
Street markets, boot sales and junkshops are cheapest but beware of
obviously under-priced bikes particularly if they are quite new. Aside
from moral considerations you may be spotted by its former owner.
Check to see if the machine is security marked or post-coded in any
way.

The local press carry some bikes; better quality machines will be in the
classified columns of bicycle magazines, or on noticeboards in bike
shops. If all else fails ask your friends, neighbours and colleagues if they
know of any unwanted bikes. There are many perfectly suitable bikes
gathering dust in garages and hallways waiting for you to make an
offer.

When buying a secondhand bike you must be confident that you can
spot the kind of serious faults which turn a bargain into a lemon. Enlist
the help of a competent cyclist if you can find one willing. Otherwise
use this check list. The best way to familiarise yourself with it is to
borrow a bike and practice all the checks on it. You could even go to a
bike shop and try them on a test-ride machine.

Buyers checklist.

1. Check the frame for cracks or bends, look where the tubes are joined and around the drop-outs (the slots where the wheels go). Wrinkles in the metal or cracked paint can betray crash damage. Look closely at the top of the down-tube and the front of the top-tube, the most likely place for it.

2. Is everything fastened on tightly? Are the wheels secure in the frame? Check the seat and handlebars, the control levers for brakes and gears, any mudguards, bottle-cages, bells, lights and luggage racks.

3. Spin the wheels and bottom-bracket axle. Any clicks or drags mean the bearings are too tight. Try and pull each wheel rim and the crank arms from side to side. If there is any 'play' the bearings are too loose. It may well be possible to rectify these faults with small adjustments but they may require more serious repair.

4. The steering should move freely from side to side but not be too loose. Check the headset for looseness by turning the front wheel at 90 degrees to the frame and then rocking the bike back and forward. You will feel if there is any movement between the frame and forks.

5. Check the wheel rims for buckles by spinning the wheels and watching where they pass the brakes. Small (5mm) side to side movements are easily cured, up and down wobbles are more serious.

6. Check the tyres for holes and splits. Blow them up to the correct pressure check again for splits and bulges.

7. Pull the brakes hard. The levers should travel no more than 50 mm. and you should be able to get two fingers between the lever and the handlebars. The brake blocks should hit the metal wheel rim and not touch the tyre. Release the brakes and check the wheels spin freely.

8. Check the cables for fraying, especially brake cables inside the lever. Are the outer cables kinked or damaged?

9. Ride the bike. Do all the gears engage without trouble and propel the bike without slipping or making grinding or clicking noises. If the bike has derailleur gears pay particular attention to the extremes of the range; the biggest front wheel to smallest rear (top) and smallest front to biggest rear (bottom). Listen for rattles - a double-check against any loose components.

10. Make turns in either direction. They should feel the same. Ride no-handed or holding the bars very lightly. The bike should not veer right or left. If it pulls to one side the frame may be bent.

If you notice any faults the vendor may try and reassure you that they are minor. In that case ask them to rectify them for you or get an estimate for repair from a shop. In this way you will find out if the bike needs any expensive or rare replacement parts.

Fitting.
You should be able to stand astride the top-tube (cross bar) with both feet flat on the floor. If you plan to use it for rough off-road riding where occasional falls are likely a further gap of around 50 mm decreases the risk of injury. The range of bicycles for short people is limited because frames are built to accommodate wheels of a standard size. Short people should look for a frame with a sloping top tube which will let them stand across it.

The seat height is adjusted by loosening the clamp at the top of the seat-tube and sliding the seat-post up or down. The clamp is held tight by a bolt, released with a spanner or allen key, or a quick-release lever which lets you adjust the seat without tools.

The seat height should be sufficient to allow you to pedal easily with the balls of your feet. A simple test is to sit in the seat, with someone holding you up or while leaning on a wall, place your heels on the pedals. When the pedal is furthest from the seat your leg should be straight, but with the knee not quite locked-out. Put the balls of your feet on the pedals and back-pedal; you should be able to spin easily without rocking your pelvis. The seat-post has a warning line on it - do not raise it above this point. If you need more height you need a longer post. They are not of standard diameter so take the old post or the cycle to your bike shop.

Start with the seat level, some riders (mostly men) like their seat tipped slightly back to stop them slipping forward when they pedal hard, others (mostly women) find it more comfortable with the nose of the seat angled slightly down. The distance from seat to handlebars should be about the length of your fore-arm from elbow to finger tip. This can be adjusted by sliding the seat backwards or forwards. The height of the bars can be adjusted by unscrewing the nut on top of the handlebar-stem, and tapping it down to release the stem. The handlebar-stem also has a warning line showing the minimum insertion required.

During the first months you may want to experiment with your position. Move the seat or bars no more than 10mm at a time and give yourself a fortnight to get used to each position. Putting the handlebars high puts more weight on your seat. As a general rule your bars should be no higher than your seat if this is uncomfortable start with the bars up to 50mm higher, and lower them over a period of time as your back, neck and arms get stronger.

The saddle on your bike should be wide enough to support your pelvic bones rather than the soft bits in between but otherwise don't worry if you find your seat gets uncomfortable after a short distance at first. As your legs get stronger they will be able to take more of your weight for longer distances. If after a few months you still find your seat uncomfortable you may need to shop around for one which is a different shape. Women's saddles are usually shorter and broader at the back than men's saddles. There are a range of different types of saddles - leather covered, nylon covered etc - look at the selection in a bike shop.

Gearing.

Before the invention of the roller chain the pedals of a bike were linked directly to the front wheel and the only way to alter the ratio of pedalling speed to road speed was by making the drive wheel bigger. This lead to the high bicycle or 'penny-farthing'. The advent of the rear wheel driven safety bicycle allowed a gearing ratio to be selected to suit the needs and abilities of the rider. The invention of a variable speed transmission followed soon after so the rider could select a gear appropriate to the conditions while travelling.

For a novice rider with reasonable fitness a single speed bike is perfectly adequate. Its simplicity means less weight and fewer things to go wrong. Most bikes sold today have variable speed systems to allow the rider to deal more efficiently with a range of conditions, hills, winds, rough surfaces, luggage or fatigue. Bikes with more than one gear use either hub gears or derailleur systems to select them. Each has its own advantages and drawbacks.

Hub gears.

A hub gear system has the mechanism enclosed in a metal cylinder at the centre of the rear wheel. It requires minimum maintenance and has a service life of thirty years or more. The gears can be changed while the bike is stationary which makes it easy to use in traffic. The standard three speed system the 'Sturmey Archer AW' has gears rather wide apart for efficient cruising and the extremes of the range are limited, but models with five or more speeds are available. In Britain hub gears have become unfashionable. In Northern Europe where much more utility and non-athletic leisure cycling is undertaken they are popular and not considered to be an inferior option. A few of these machines are imported here and some British manufacturers offer a hub gear option on certain models. If your priorities are low maintenance and reliability it is worth searching out a quality bike with hub gears.

Derailleur Gears.

This system allows a much wider choice of speeds. With lots of gears close together so you can pick your cruising speed exactly or a broad range of speeds suitable for efficient riding in conditions from steep muddy tracks to level tarmac. Derailleur gears work because the chain runs on a range of different sized, uncovered, cog wheels. These works need to be lubricated and the lubricant picks up dirt. To work well and prolong their life they need regular cleaning and relubrication but even with the best attention the moving parts have a short service life.

The 'indexed' derailleur mechanisms on modern bikes are very easy to operate but you still need to be moving to change gear and the sophistication of the systems means they need more cleaning, adjustment and replacement of parts.

Accessories

Mudguards

Your bike should be fitted with mudguards. It is one thing to be soaked by rain - something which happens surprisingly rarely in South East England - it is another to have dirty water jetted up your nose and tail. The only exception to this rule is if you plan to ride the off-road in muddy conditions. Here mudguards (unless there is a large clearance between the tyre and the mudguards) can soon jam up with mud and leaves rendering your bike not only unridable but probably unpushable too.

Luggage

A minimum of personal effects - wallet, keys, puncture repair kit, banana can be carried in a rucksack or bum-bag anything more than this should be fixed to the bike. A handlebar bag or small saddle bag is ideal for day trips. Buying cheap luggage is a false economy but equally the most expensive 'expedition' type gear is not necessary for gentle cycle touring. Go for quality rather than tricky features and your luggage should give many years of reliable service. If you want to ride off road pay particular attention to the way the luggage is fixed on. Some systems will stay put during prolonged bouncing, others will not.

Lights

If you plan to ride all year round or make extended night rides in Summer the best lighting system is a tyre driven dynamo. These are cheap, the simplest cost little more than a set of battery lights and one set of batteries. They are 'green' and are less likely to let you down than battery lights, carry a spare bulb. A dynamo set weighs less than battery lights and cannot readily be stolen. You can supplement them with an L.E.D. (light emitting diode) rear light if you are worried about your lights going out when you are stationary. L.E.D. lights are very bright, small and their batteries last a long time. It is worth carrying them whenever there is a risk that your journey will be prolonged after dark. If you are going into unfamiliar country in the dark and have dynamo lighting a small pencil torch is useful for map reading.

Clothing

It is quite possible to ride a bike in everyday clothes but cycle clothing works and from the wide range available you should be able to find something that fits your image. The most important items are shorts, gloves and shoes, in that order. These will improve your comfort and performance so much that once you've tried them you will be reluctant to ride in anything else.

Gloves

Finger-less padded gloves (called track mitts) protect your hands from shocks which means you can put more weight on your arms and less on your bottom. They will also save your palms in the event of a fall. Even in Summer, evenings and mornings can chill your fingers, especially going downhill. A pair of light thermal glove liners take up very little room and can be more use than an extra jersey.

Shoes

When you ride a bike you generate power with the big muscles in your back and thighs. This power has to be transmitted to the pedals through your feet which are quite delicate with lots of small bones and soft-tissue. If you wear soft shoes designed for walking your feet will soon become tired and sore and the shoes will wear out prematurely. Cycling shoes are reinforced with metal, wood or composite material to support your foot and allow better use of your leg muscles. Pure cycling shoes are uncomfortable to walk any distance in and this will also reduce their rigidity. Trainer type cycling shoes which are good for cycling and OK for walking are the best compromise for the casual tourist. Wearing shoes designed for cycling will support your knees and ankles and by helping you push power through your legs keep the weight off your bottom.

Toe-clips and system pedals

With smooth soled shoes you can use toe-clips. These gadgets, feared by many novices, encourage a fluid pedalling style and give the rider more control over the bike. It takes a few hours to get used to using them but they make riding much easier. Even better are the modern systems based on ski-binding technology which anchor your feet on the pedals with sprung catches. With these you can pull up on the pedals hard but a small twist of the foot is all that is needed to pull your foot free. At present these systems are expensive - you have to buy new shoes as well as pedals.

Shorts or tights

Shorts made of tight stretchy material cut out friction between you and the bike and they contain a padded seat. You can also buy padded underwear to use under ordinary clothes. If you ride in non-cycle shorts or trousers they should have no bulky seams at the crotch which will feel like the Andes when you have been sitting on them for an hour or two. In cool weather tights or tracksuit-bottoms can be worn over padded shorts. Leg warmers are useful on days which change from winter to summer in the blink of an eye.

Rainwear

A breathable waterproof doubles as an extra layer of warmth but these garments are costly and sweaty individuals find they can't prevent moisture build-up. If you use a simple waterproof jacket check it does not obstruct your pedalling. In summer conditions over-trousers are more trouble than they are worth. In practice it is virtually impossible to keep dry while cycling in heavy rain. Once you are soaked, so long as you can keep warm, rain ceases to be a problem. In an emergency plastic bags will keep your hands and feet warm and a newspaper up your jumper will keep the wind off your chest.

Other clothing
Although cycling can be hot work, moving quickly through the air can chill you even on a warm day. It is useful to have clothing with vents and zips so you can keep cool going uphill and warm going down. Thin layers give warmth and allow precise regulation in changing conditions. Upper body clothing should be long enough to keep your lower back warm even when you are leaning forward over the bars. A small scarf and hat can provide the warmth of an extra jersey for less bulk. If you don't wear a helmet a light coloured sun-hat will keep the sun off your head and keep the sweat out of your eyes on hills.

Bulky clothing will slow you down by adding wind resistance, a flapping jacket can add 20% to the effort required to make progress. That is why jockeys wear silk shirts. Purpose made cycling jerseys have pockets out of the way at the back for cameras, snacks, maps, etc. Having them instantly available saves energy and they keep your jersey down over your kidneys.

Hard hats
Cycle helmets are designed to protect your head in an impact of up to 12 mph. They will not necessarily protect your head in a crash with a fast moving, motor-vehicle. If you do bang your head you will certainly be glad of one. They are very light. The two practical arguments against their use are that they can be uncomfortably hot in summer (get a white one) and that it is one more piece of luggage to carry around when you are not riding. If you choose to wear one make sure it fits well. It should stay in place when you shake your head vigorously even without the chin-strap closed.

Unfortunately the 'road safety' lobby have taken up helmets for cyclists as an important issue. This piece of victim blaming reinforces a false perception of cycling as a very hazardous activity. It has meant that political considerations now influence some people in an area that should be left to personal choice, and that statistical conclusions concerning the value of hard-hats vary depending on whether the researcher wants to prove they are helpful or useless. When the Minister for Roads and Traffic said helmets for cyclists would become compulsory when the majority of cyclist wore them voluntarily, many long term helmet users stopped wearing them.

When a fall is most expected, in freezing weather or during tricky off-road riding it is sensible to wear one. It is not necessary for an adult to wear a helmet to ride a bike, it is a matter of personal choice. It is sensible for young children to wear a helmet.

Bikes & cars

A bike without mudguards and with the wheels removed can fit into the boot of a large saloon car or on the back seat of a smaller one. If you want to carry bikes on the outside a boot-rack is the simplest way of doing this. These fit quickly onto almost any vehicle using hooks and compression straps and carry two or three bikes. They fold flat and can be stored easily when not in use. If the bikes or the rack obscure the number plate you are obliged to fit an extra plate (with a light at night) outside the bikes.

Of roof-rack systems the easiest to use are those where the front wheel is removed and the front forks clamped on a dummy hub. If you use one remember not to drive under any low gateways.

Security

One thing you may be able to do without on a leisure ride is a heavy 'D' lock which is essential for inner-city parking. Use a lighter cable-lock or even better park your bike where you can overlook it if you are stopping for food and drink. Not everyone in a party needs to carry a lock.

Insurance

Cycle insurance is expensive reflecting the frequency of cycle theft. Fashionable mountain bikes are attractive to thieves. Many policies refuse insurance to residents of certain city centre post-codes or impose surcharges for bikes with flat handlebars. The high cost of insurance has lead many cyclists to trust only strong locks, others use low-cost, low-status hack bikes for the kind of journeys which involve unsupervised parking and only take their nice bikes out when they can sit on, or watch them all the time.

If you have a household contents policy adding your bike to it can be the cheapest way to insure it. Membership of the BCF (British Cycling Federation) LCC, CTC or ETA gives you access to specific cycle insurance policies and also gives you free third party liability (you're covered for damage you cause to others and their property) and legal aid cover.

MAINTAINING YOUR BIKE

Clean It.

There are several good arguments for cleaning your bike regularly. How regularly depends on how dirty you get it. Real mud-pups will need to clean their bikes after almost every ride. If you ride only on roads in good weather once or twice a year will do. Keeping a bike clean will prolong the life of the paint and moving parts. The cleaning process is a good opportunity to check the bike thoroughly. You won't get dirty when riding, or maintaining a clean bike. A clean bike is easier to store and transport. When it is clean you can relubricate it. If you have to take it to the bike shop clean it first and you will get quicker more attentive service. If you are worried about attracting thieves disguise the bike in ways other than keeping it filthy, with a rust or mud coloured paint, or tape, or even better avoid parking in high risk areas.

How to clean a bike.

Cleaning a bike is not a difficult job. The first time you do it will take an hour or more but you will soon develop a confident routine. The best time to clean your bike is straight after a wet ride before the grime has had time to dry. If you can find a hook, branch or washing line to hang the bike from, the job will be easier. If you have quick release wheels (levers that clamp the wheel in the frame) rather than hexagonal nuts - or if the bike is very dirty, remove them (see Punctures).

Brush degreaser on the lubricated parts - the chain, cog-wheels and gear (use either hydro-carbon based solvent - white spirit is cleaner than petrol or paraffin but they will suffice. Toxic, water-soluble solvents like 'Gunk' or 'Jizer' work but are very nasty chemicals. The best are non-toxic biodegradable versions like Finish Line Citrus. They are expensive but work very well in small quantities.) Use water on the rest. How much water and whether you apply it with a sponge, a hand-pumped bottle or a damp rag depends on how dirty the bike is. Work from the top down. The water will not harm the bike if you let it dry thoroughly afterwards.

By the time you get down to the transmission (the chain), the degreaser should have loosened the grease. Rinse with soapy water for water-soluble degreasers or more of the same for white spirit or petrol. Rinse the bike with clean water using a sponge or damp cloth.

When the bike is dry you can wax polish it. This protects the paint and builds up a hard film. When the bike gets dirty again the dirt is on the polish and not the bike so it will be easier to clean next time. This is the time to check the frame (see notes on secondhand bikes).

Lubricate it.

When you are sure they are dry lubricate the moving parts sparingly with synthetic lubricant. This is expensive but if you use a brush (not an aerosol which is terribly wasteful and messy) a little goes a long way. Run the lube into the cable housing where the inner cables emerge. Wipe off any excess immediately as it will only attract dirt. If you have the bike hanging off the ground you can spin the wheels and check the operation of the gears and brakes.

Synthetic lubricants come in a variety of grades the lightest (e.g.WD40) are clean but need frequent reapplication particularly in wet conditions. The stickier kind (e.g. Finish Line Century Lube, Green Mountain Bike Lube) never dry so they remain in place longer but they also attract dirt so should be cleaned off before further lubrication is added. A few layers of grit and oil on a bike chain will stop it going rusty but also act as a grinding paste to quickly reduce your chainwheel teeth to stumps.

Check it.

Regular cleaning and taking your bike to the shop if you find anything suspect, will hone your diagnostic skills. (Use the notes on secondhand bikes for guidance.) These are important because loose parts wear out very quickly so even a few miles riding can turn a minor maladjustment into a costly repair. If you find anything suspect get it checked. Bicycle mechanics are based on a few simple principles and can be easily mastered by anyone willing to spend a little time. The basic tools are inexpensive. If you have bad memories of trying to fix bikes in the past remember working on a good quality bike with the correct tools makes a big difference. (see Training for information on maintenance classes). If you think your life is already complex enough and you prefer to pay a professional mechanic you should still learn to diagnose faults and mend punctures. Without these simple skills you will never be able to use your bike with full confidence.

Accept the inevitable.
Check your tyres weekly and change them before they let you down far
from home. Get the bike shop to check your chain for wear at least
every three months, they should have a gauge to do this in 10 seconds.
If you ride with a worn chain it will wear the rest of the transmission
system. If you ride your bike the tyres and chain WILL wear out.
Bicycles are cheap to run but not free. Changing tyres and chain in good
time will save time, trouble and money in the long run.

Punctures.
Mending punctures has been part of cycle travel since the invention of
the pneumatic tyre. Good tyres and a little preventive action make them
very a rare occurrence but if you ride your bike sooner or later you will
have one. Changing a tube is not a difficult job and the tools are light
enough to carry everywhere. As with any skill, practice and confidence
are the keys to success. Mending your first puncture will be stressful.
The tenth will be nothing more than a short unscheduled stop.

Mending a puncture can be divided into 4 phases.
1. Removing and replacing the wheel.
2. Tracing and removing the source of the puncture.
3. Changing the tube.
4. Mending the tube.

1. To remove the wheel first open the brake if necessary. Then pull the
quick release lever to the open position or loosen the nuts. Drop the
front wheel from the frame by tapping the tyre hard with your hand.
For derailleur rear wheels run the chain to the smallest combination of
cog wheels, loosen the axle, then stand behind the bike, pull the gear
mechanism back with your right fingers while pushing the axle forward
with your thumbs. The wheel will drop out. Unhook the freewheel from
the chain.

For three speed rear wheels unscrew the control chain, loosen the nuts
and push the wheel forward and down.

2. Once the tyre is off the rim on one side (see no. 3) you can pull the
tube out. Blow it up with the valve still in the rim and listen for the hiss
of escaping air. If you can locate the hole in the tube with the valve still
in the rim you can trace the source of the puncture quickly. If you can't
find the hole by sight or sound get it away from the rim blow it up and
run it past your face and feel for the jet of air. Check the valve with spit.
The smallest, slowest punctures are the hardest to find.

When you have found the hole, match the tube to the wheel and tyre and look in the area where the hole was. If you don't know which way round the tube was you must look in one of two areas - unless the hole is dead opposite the valve. Check the tyre for grit, glass, thorns or nails. Check for holes where they may have been. Run your fingers carefully inside the tyre to feel for the sharp point. Pick out whatever caused the puncture - tweezers or a pin may be useful. The puncture may also have been made by the end of a spoke so check the rim tape and file down any high spokes. In an emergency you can pad the spokes with strong glossy paper or a scrap of tough cloth.

A puncture can be caused by hitting a kerb, a stone or a pothole. These often come in a symmetrical pair and are known as 'snake bite' punctures. This can be a sign that your tyres were under inflated. Another source of punctures is if the tube was installed with a twist or fold in which case the hole will lie on a bigger crease mark. If the tyre is very worn or badly cut replace it. If it is not worn but has a bad cut you can patch it with a home-made patch, stick the patch with contact cement or as a temporary roadside resort rubber solution. If the cut is big it may need a stitch or two to hold the patch in place and keep it closed. Small cuts can be mended with super glue.

3. To change the tube, find the valve (where the air goes in), make sure the tube is fully deflated and remove the lock-ring if present. Pinch the tyre to unstick it from the rim. You may be able to pull it off the rim by hand otherwise use levers to prize it off. Push the first one under. Push another one under then pull them both down. Take care, they can fly out. If the tyre still won't come off try a third lever. If it still won't, take out the middle one to make a fourth. Leave the tyre half on the rim and pull out the tube, the valve comes out last. When you are sure the source of the puncture is traced and removed (see no. 2) put a new tube in. Install the valve first. Putting a little bit of air in it helps to get it in without twists or folds. Dusting it with talcum powder will help it move inside the tyre and prevent 'snake bites'.

Work the tyre bead back onto the rim with your fingers. Tools can puncture the tube. If it is very tight, work the rest of the bead into the bottom of the rim and stretch any slack round to where you are working. Talc will help it slide over the rim if it is tight. When the tyre is back on push the valve seat up inside the tyre. Inflate the tube lightly and check it is not trapped by the tyre and that the tyre bead is seated evenly on the rim.

On some bikes the rear wheels won't go back in the frame with air in the tyre but it is usually easier to blow the tyre up before you put the wheel back in. Pump using a full stroke. Grip the pump on the valve with one hand and push hard with the other. Count the strokes and think about something that makes you angry. Reinstall the wheel and close the brake. (reverse no.1).

4. Mending a punctured tube is a fiddly job but even if you don't plan to do it as a matter of course it is a good idea to learn. Carry at least one spare tube. Find the hole using the procedure above plus as a last resort a bowl of water and look for bubbles. Mark the hole with pen or clothes peg. When the tube is dry lightly roughen the area round the hole with fine sandpaper. If an old patch has failed tear it off and remove the old glue. Put a coat of glue, bigger than the patch round the hole. Let it dry. How long depends on the temperature, humidity and wind. You cannot leave it too long. When the glue is dry to the touch and you can no longer smell alcohol evaporating peel the backing from the patch (if it has paper and foil it is the foil covered side that sticks to the tube) and press it over the hole. If you have lost the hole while the glue dried a little air in the tube will show you where it is. If the patch also had a paper backing on the top, peel that off carefully.

Puncture tools.
A pump to fit your valves.
Spanners to remove wheels if they are not quick release.
Tyre levers.
Spare tube(s).
A puncture repair kit.
Extra tools for remote trips and home workshop:-
Contact cement - sandpaper - pin -tweezers - small file home-made emergency tyre patches* - nail scissors - super glue - big needle and a sail-makers palm for pushing it - strong thread.

*Prepare patches by cutting useful sizes - between 10 x 30 mm and 20 x 60mm depending on your tyre size - from the fabric side-walls of old tyres. Give one side a coat of contact glue and let it dry.

Prevention of punctures.
Keep your tyres at the correct pressure - embossed on the tyre wall - and change them when they become worn. Use strong tyres reinforced with Kevlar, a space age bullet proof material. Check your tyres regularly for foreign bodies and remove grit and glass before it can work through to the tube.

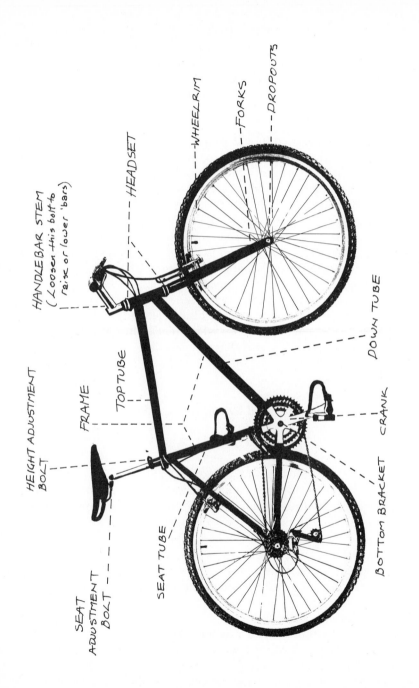

HANDLE BAR STEM
(Loosen this bolt to raise or lower 'bars)

HEADSET

WHEEL RIM

FORKS

DROPOUTS

DOWN TUBE

TOP TUBE

HEIGHT ADJUSTMENT BOLT

FRAME

CRANK

SEAT ADJUSTMENT BOLT

SEAT TUBE

BOTTOM BRACKET

Each month BIKE 1 offers a new one day cycle ride in a different English county. The rides allow you to cycle at your own pace with full back up, and include a meal at the end of your day's cycling. Whichever rides you choose, you can look forward to a truly enjoyable and trouble-free day's cycling, with

- **Food & Drink included**
- **Choice of routes**
- **Mechanic & First Aid**
- **Quiet country routes**

- **Start when you like**
- **Fully signposted**
- **Telephone Helpline**
- **Easy train access**

At Bike 1 we believe cycling is not just about excellent routes; it's also about good food and great company. We take care of the routes, provide all the back up and food, you provide the great company! The friendly atmosphere in the hall after you've had a great days cycling really is a memorable part of your day - you'll probably find yourself lingering and exchanging stories for some time!

SUSTRANS

We support the work of SUSTRANS - the cycle route construction charity who have a 1,000 mile Dover to Inverness cycle route planned.

To ensure that the rides are most enjoyable we have a limit of around 250 riders for each County Day Ride. So to avoid disappointment **CALL TODAY** for a free information pack on all our rides including our SUSTRANS events. Write, phone or fax.

"The organisation, reception, food, and air of friendliness was second to none ...many thanks for a most enjoyable day." P. Fewtrell

BIKE 1
PO Box 105
Fleet, Hampshire
GU13 8YR
0252 624942 FAX
0252 624022 TEL

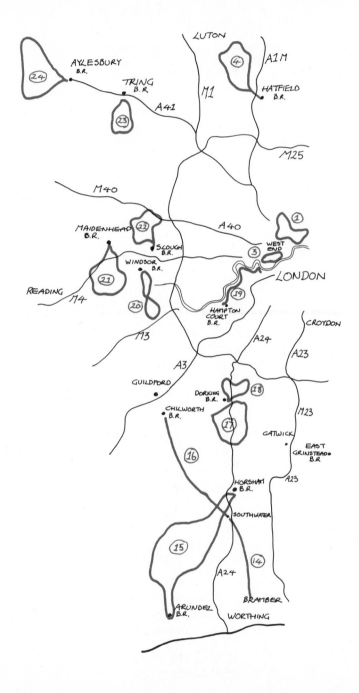

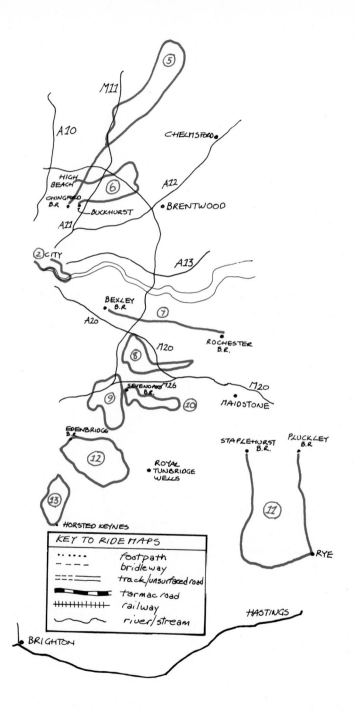

LONDON'S PARKS & GREEN CORRIDORS VIA HAMPSTEAD HEATH

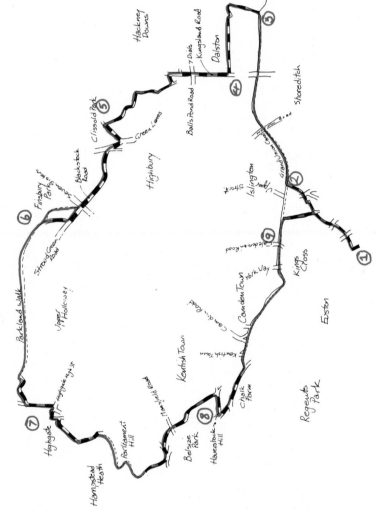

LONDON'S PARKS & GREEN CORRIDORS
VIA HAMPSTEAD HEATH

Map	London Street Atlas. OS LR 176 West London Area will give you the shape but is not much use for intricate route finding.
Start	Lamb's Conduit Street in Bloomsbury WC1 has minimum motor-traffic and the Lamb and the Sun pubs are good places to meet. It is close to Euston, Kings Cross and St. Pancras and accessible from the other London Termini.
Finish	Lamb's Conduit Street in Bloomsbury WC1.
Distance	15.5 miles
Route	The route takes back streets out of Central London, picks up the Regents Canal in Islington, follows it to Hackney then climbs via Finsbury Park and the green corridor of the Parkland Walk to Hampstead Heath. After crossing the Heath it returns to the Canal at Camden and from there back to Islington.
Attractions	Regents Canal, Chapel Market, London Fields, the Parkland Walk, Hampstead Heath, Parliament Hill, Camden Market.
Refreshments	A myriad of street cafe's, restaurants and pubs to choose from.

Lambs Conduit Street (1) is traffic calmed, one- way for motors but two- way for bikes. A little bit of the Netherlands in London. The bicycle repair shop at number 48 is open until 19:00 on weekdays.

Leave the street by its north end, directly opposite is Coram Fields, a nice park that you can only enter if you are accompanied by a child. Turn right into Guildford Street, which becomes Calthorpe Street as it crosses the Grays Inn Road. At the next lights fork left up the steep Lloyd Baker Street.

The area on top of this Hill is New River Head. Where Hugh Myddelton's canal, which brought clean drinking water from the Lea Valley in Hertfordshire to the cholera prone city, had its terminus. Before the canal, water was either brought up from the Thames in carts or came in local wooden pipes, which are commemorated where 'conduit' appears in a street name. The New River allowed London to expand northwards onto areas of clay with few natural springs or streams. The Thames Water Board still has its headquarters in the area, although now the New River terminates in Clissold Park.

Cross Amwell Street into River Street and go round Myddleton Square to Chadwell Street. Go straight over at the lights and cross Goswell Road and City Road on the cycle- track into Colebrooke Row.

The hilltop area to the left is known as the Angel Islington after a coaching inn - the first landmark on the Great North Road. There are two street markets in this area. Chapel Market just across Upper Street and Camden Passage on its Eastern side.

Turn right down Vincent Terrace, left over the canal and right down a ramp (2) (1.5 miles) to join the towpath. This is the Regents Canal which links the Grand Union at Brentford to the River Lea and the Docks at Limehouse. It has just emerged from a tunnel under Islington.

Technically you need a permit to cycle on this path but very few riders have one and those who do are never asked to produce it. It is a leisure route for pedestrians so ride carefully particularly near bridges and other blind corners and pass pedestrians at walking pace. On your right are Eagle Wharf, Wenlock and City Road Basins.

At the third lock (3) (3 miles) emerge and turn right and left to enter Broadway Market where flowers and plants are sold on Saturdays. (Turning south and following the cycle track will take you down to Brick Lane to join the WEST END TO DOCKLANDS ride). On the left is Frederick Cooke's live eel shop where you can enjoy this local delicacy.

At the top of Broadway Market use the light-controlled crossing to enter London Fields. As you reach the interchange of cycle paths, you can inspect the Hackney Empire and pick up a programme of forthcoming events at the flamboyant old musical hall by going straight ahead along Martello Street and Hackney Grove for a quarter of a mile. Otherwise, turn left signposted for Islington.

Leave London Fields for Middleton Road. You are now following the Maurice Hope cycle route named after the Light- Middleweight Champion of the World 1979- 81 (Hackney and Antigua) who is reputed to have done his road work on these streets. After passing under the railway bridge turn right (4) (4 miles) onto the Kingsland Road.

The Waste, a bustling market operates here on Saturdays with lots of interesting junk. On the right is Faulkners, a very good fish and chip shop. Cross the busy Dalston Junction. A first right after this, Abbot Street, takes you to the Green Door Café in Ashwin Street with good vegetarian food and bike parking.

Dalston's other attraction is Ridley Road Market which on Fridays and Saturdays is one of London's best, selling fruit and vegetables, shoes and clothing. The market, another right turn off the Kingsland Road opposite Dalston Kingsland BR station, has a 24 hour bakery and delicatessen which, in the small hours, is the most like Manhattan that London ever gets.

Turn left by the Rio Cinema and right at the traffic lights into Boleyn Road. Turn right into Wordsworth Road then left into Allen Road and right into Milton Grove. Cross Albion Road into Clissold Road. At the end of Clissold road turn right (5) (6 miles) if you want to visit Stoke Newington Church Street and the back gate into the gothic wilderness of Abney Park Cemetery.

Otherwise turn left then right into Green Lanes, the longest road with one name in London, and left after the Whitehouse pub into Riversdale Road. Fork right into Mountgrove Road and then turn right into Finsbury Park Road. At the end of this, cross the busy Seven Sisters Road into Finsbury Park.

The Park is closed after dark so then you must walk round the corner on your left to find the winding path just past the bowling alley in Stroud Green

Road. Ride up through the park keeping to the left. At the tennis courts, turn left over the narrow metal bridge across the railway (the night route rejoins just before the bridge) over the bridge turn sharp right (6) (7 miles) to join the Parkland Walk.

This length of abandoned rail trackbed is one of north London's treasures. Its steady gradient allows you to climb easily through the trees past the abandoned stations. When the path terminates in a blocked tunnel, climb to your left and emerge into Holmesdale Road.

Turn right and right onto the A1 Archway - the Great North Road - and make an immediate left up Jacksons Lane. At the top turn left and follow the one- way system round to take the third exit, Hampstead Lane. Take the first left (7) (10 miles) into The Grove, where Coleridge once lived, and turn right into the private roadway Fitzroy Park.

This long descent with speed bumps brings you to Millfield by Hampstead Heath. Turn onto the Heath where the cycle track is marked. Men may swim in the pool to the left. The Women's pond is higher up to the right in a nicer wooded setting.

Take the path straight on uphill. On your left is Parliament Hill with a long view across

London to Crystal Palace. This is a popular place for kite flying and sledging when snow falls. When the path levels out among trees, turn left and follow it down, keeping right to cross another flight of ponds. The one on your right is for mixed bathing.

Turn left to come into South End Green, keep left into Agincourt Road and at the bottom go over into Southampton Road. Fork left into Malden Road.

At the bottom turn right into Prince of Wales Road and left (8) (12.5 miles) into Chalk Farm Road. Marine Ices on your left serves acceptable Italian food and wonderful ice creams. Carry on down the road (the bike shop at number 44 is open 7 days a week). In the one- way system at the bottom, dismount and go straight on. Fashionable Camden Lock market gets very busy at weekends. Turn right onto the canal and double back under Chalk Farm Road.

The canal (which here is closed after dark) takes you through the railway lands behind Kings Cross where the Camley Street Nature reserve has been built and plans to build a giant office complex have collapsed. The Gasometers are painted in the livery of their original owners, the Metropolitan Gas Company.

When the canal enters the Islington Tunnel, emerge to cross Caledonian Road (9) (14 miles) and walk up past the children's playground following the path the towing-horses once used to find Maygood Street. Turn right onto Barnsbury Road and follow this back to New River Head.

To return to Lambs Conduit Street (1) (15.5 miles) retrace your route except for Lloyd Baker Street which is one- way. Margery Street, the next turning on the right, provides an alternative.

THE WEST END TO DOCKLANDS

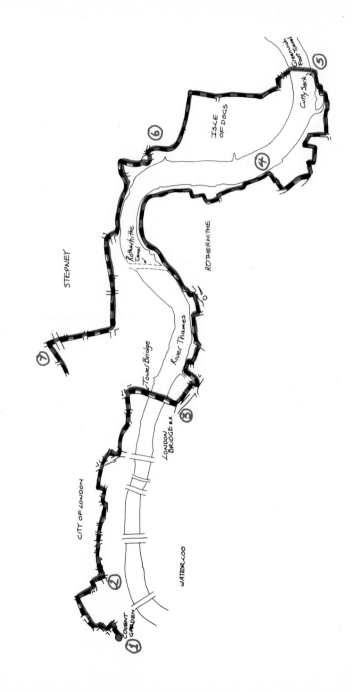

THE WEST END TO DOCKLANDS

Map	London Street Atlas. OS LR 177 East London Area will give you the shape but is not much use for intricate route finding.
Start	Covent Garden is easily reached from all London Termini and Thameslink.
Finish	Brick Lane, Spitalfields.
Distance	15 miles. The only hill is the one on which the City of London stands.
Route	The route begins in the West End, slips by the Inns of Court into the City of London, over Tower Bridge and through the riverside hamlets of Bermondsey, Rotherhithe and Deptford to Greenwich. North through the architectural zoo of the Isle of Dogs to return to the Old East End in Spitalfields.
Attractions	Covent Garden. the City, Tower of London, The Design Centre, Greenwich, Canary Wharf.
Refreshments	Tea and Coffee Museum on Shad Thames Street and plenty of cafés and pubs in Greenwich.

Covent Garden was originally an open courtyard like the Plaza Major in Madrid, a 17th Century building on former convent lands. By the 18th Century the wealthy and aristocratic had moved further west and the place had become a known for theatres, gambling and prostitution, the kind of low-life which has never been tolerated in the City of London. The neighbourhood's decline in status was accelerated by a ramshackle market in flowers, fruits and vegetables which grew up in the square. In 1830 the building in the centre of the piazza was built to house the market which operated until 1974.

Leave the Piazza (1) eastwards down Russell Street. Notice the Theatre Royal ahead and right. Even the back looks grand. Turn left up Bow Street. The Royal Opera on your left has played host to almost as many famous names as the Magistrates Court and Police Station (no longer operational) on your right.

Turn right along Broad Court, giving way to pedestrians. Turn left into Drury Lane and right into Great Queen Street, a continuation of Long Acre - the convent garden's northern boundary.

Cross the Kingsway - built in the late 19th Century to relieve traffic congestion in Drury Lane and

Chancery Lane, into Remnant Street. Lincoln's Inn Fields used to be a pleasant stop but is now fenced to prevent homeless people camping there. The Inns of Court, of which Lincoln's Inn is one, grew up in the space between the licentious West End and the staid and puritanical City, as hostels where lawyers were trained. They still house the legal profession.

Go along the square passing on your left the Sir John Soane Museum which is crammed full of his collected treasures. Turn right at the corner of the square. Pass the entrance to Lincoln's Inn itself into Serle Street. Ahead are the Royal Courts of Justice - the Old Bailey. Turn left, then right into Bell Yard. At the bottom of Bell Yard walk across the pavement to join Fleet Street at Temple Bar (2) (1 mile) the Western limit of the City of London. Turn left. Long before newspapers, Fleet Street was famous for its debtors' prison.

Ahead St. Paul's comes into view. From most aspects Wren's great landmark is dwarfed by office blocks, but approached up Ludgate Hill it still looks mighty. At Ludgate Circus the route crosses the line of the River Fleet, which rises as a spring on Hampstead Heath, and was long ago channelled into underground pipes. On your right on Ludgate Hill is Blackfriars Thameslink BR

Station, an alternative starting point.

Keep to the right of St. Pauls and once past it turn left into New Change and right into Watling Street, which is one-way but it is worth the trouble this causes to pass along the most significant road in Britain. Watling Street runs from Dover to Chester, and London has grown up where it crosses the Thames. These narrow streets give a rare clue to the character of the City before blitz and developers struck.

Turn left into Bow Lane. On a summer Friday night when the office workers drink on the street you will have to walk up here and at anytime it requires care. Turn right onto Cheapside, the main market of Mediaeval London. On the left is the Bank of England. Fork slightly right into Lombard Street. The Lombards from Northern Italy started London's banking tradition in the 12th Century and this area is still full of banks from all over the world.

Turn right into Clements Lane and left into King William Street. Pass the end of London Bridge, which takes Watling Street over the river and becomes the Old Kent Road to Canterbury, Dover and Europe. It is around 1500 years since the Romans built the first wooden bridge on this site.

The present bridge was opened in 1972. Its predecessor was sold and re-erected in Arizona.

Go straight on into Eastcheap. On your right you can catch a glimpse of The Monument built 202 feet west of the starting point of the Great Fire of September 1666, which burned for three days and destroyed over 1300 houses. The devastation reached as far as Holborn - almost back to Covent Garden.

At the end of Eastcheap, keep right if you want to visit the Tower of London or don't like riding in uncalmed traffic. Cross to All Hallows Church and pass behind it and descend the steps. From here you can walk round the perimeter of the Tower to Tower Bridge; otherwise follow the dual carriageway left round the Tower and turn right to cross Tower Bridge.

This wild gothic fantasy, built at the end of the 19th century in steel and stone is what Arizona thought it was buying. It rarely opens now and since the new bridge was built at Dartford, no more tall masted ships can visit the centre of London. The body of water on your right between London and Tower Bridges is the Upper Pool of London. This small area was the first base of London's worldwide trade.

On the southern shore turn left (3) (4 miles) into Queen Elizabeth Street. The horse statue tells you something of the history of Bermondsey. Turn left down Shad Thames Street to find, on the riverfront, the Design Museum and the Tea and Coffee Museum which probably demands a stop at its café if you are passing in opening hours.

The way downstream is blocked by St. Saviours Dock so return to Tooley Street. The warehouses round here have been converted into apartments, offices and studios. The trade in coffee, cinnamon and nutmeg is over, but the centuries have left their mark on the bricks and the narrow streets still smell strongly of spices from the East.

Once past the Dockhead turn left again down Mill Street, follow Bermondsey Wall and Chambers Street - Bermondsey Wall East shrinks to an alley at Rotherhithe Street. Follow this line across the little park to come to the remains of the Riverside village long ago swamped by docks and housing. Follow the road over the metal bridge round Cuckolds Point. Pass the Scandia Crown Hotel and the City Farm. Keep left into Odessa Street and where it bends go straight on and turn left carefully into the alley Randalls Rents and follow the waterfront to Greenland Dock. Cross the mouth of the Dock by the road bridge past the swinging foot bridge and then cross the lock gates.

Next comes Deptford Strand (4) (7 miles) where the Royal Navy kept its stores - it is still defended by cannons. Turn inland through the Pepys Estate and then left onto Grove Street. Just before reaching the main road, turn left along the service road behind the flats. Turn right and left into Prince Street. This takes us via Benbow Street to turn right into Deptford Green where, by the Church, a faint village atmosphere persists. Turn left into the dirty lane The Stowage which brings you out into Creek Road. Turn left to cross the bridge and carry on to Greenwich (5) (8.5 miles).

Greenwich is London's gateway to the sea. Ships in the tideway set their clocks to a signal from the Royal Observatory up in Greenwich Park so they can navigate by the sun. Greenwich Mean Time is the basis for the world's time zone system and 0 degrees Longitude runs through here, putting Deptford in the Western Hemisphere and Charlton in the East. Visit Greenwich for the Cutty Sark, the Maritime Museum and the Observatory or just to wander round and enjoy the sense of history which no amount of tourists and traffic jams can erase.

To escape the summer crush follow the waterfront east from the foot-tunnel entrance to find a maze of river-front streets and the Trafalgar Tavern, The Yacht and The Cutty Sark Pubs. Sit and watch the depleted river traffic from Ballast Quay. Check the market in the centre of the towns one-way system. Go up into the park to visit the Observatory, the Maritime Museum or to picnic under the trees. Buskers perform by the dry dock which holds the tea-clipper Cutty Sark. Trains run to Charing Cross, but the river bus does not carry bikes.

Cross the river by the foot-tunnel and view the elegant symmetry of Greenwich from Islands Gardens.

From Island Gardens turn right into Ferry Street by the Docklands Light Railway, then left and right into Manchester Grove. Turn right onto East Ferry Road and follow this parallel to, and then under the DLR up into Legoland. If the Docklands Visitor Centre on the right is open, you can pick up a free street map of the area. Turn left onto Marsh Wall.

At the covered roundabout (6) (11 miles) go straight on into West Ferry Road. Pass the entry into the Docklands Highway Tunnel, reputed to be the most expensive road - per metre - ever built. Turn left into Limehouse

Causeway and follow it through Narrow Street to reach the other end of the tiny motorway. Here, taking care, turn right into the Butcher Row and then left into Cable Street.

Cable Street is to be converted into a two-way cycle route but at the time of writing remains a one-way street in places. It is famous for a battle fought in 1936. The British Union of Fascists planned to march through the East End into Aldgate, an area with a large Jewish population. Anti-fascists and local people barricaded the street and fought the police who tried to clear the way for the fascists. Eventually the Home Secretary, realising that if the march proceeded worse fighting would ensue, told the fascists leadership they could not pass. The engagement is regarded as a turning point in stopping the rise of fascism in Britain.

Turn right at the Crown and Dolphin pub into Cannon Street Road. Cross the Commercial Road and Whitechapel Road. Turn left into Old Montague Street.

In the Netherlands all streets which are one-way for motor traffic have a contra-flow for cyclists. Here the council has spent thousands on humps to slow the traffic down but cyclists are still prohibited from cycling westwards. Take care. Old Montague emerges into Osborn Street which becomes Brick Lane (7) (15 miles). The Jews have left and the next wave of immigrants are from Asia. The curry houses are plentiful and popular. The Bagel Bakery at the Bethnal Green End of the Lane is open all night.

Visit the Brick Lane Heritage Centre in Princelet Street, west of Brick Lane, - it was a Hugenot Chapel. Spitalfields was first developed as a colony of these Protestant refugees from France. It then became a synagogue and the rolls of the congregation are still written on the wooden gallery. It opens irregularly as an art gallery - if you find it open go in and enjoy. The maze of streets at the North end of Brick Lane host a busy street market from early on Sunday mornings - an excellent source of venerable old bikes.

If you follow Brick Lane North it will take you to the Market Porter's Cycle route which runs via Columbia Road and Broadway Market where it connects with the PARKS & GREEN CORRIDORS ride. To return to the West End pick your way back through the City.

Have a Blast - Rent 'n Ride

Go.ByCycle

London's Specialist Bike Rental Service
The Starting Point for *The Tourist's Track*

VISITING LONDON?
Rent a Mountain or City Bike and
discover the pleasures of sightseeing
at your own pace.

We are open Monday - Saturday
9.30-6.00

RENTALS AND SALES
Why not try before you buy?
Giant • Ridgeback • Raleigh • Trek

Just a two minute walk from Earls Court
Tube. Next to the Hotel George.

Templeton Place, Earls Court,
London SW5

071 373 3657

THE TOURIST'S TRACK

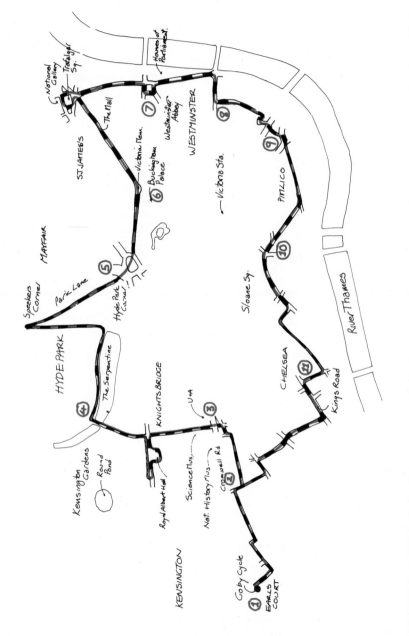

THE TOURIST'S TRACK

Map	The route map provided will give you the shape, but use a London Street Atlas for intricate route finding. supplement the route with more street detail.
Start	*Go ByCycle* in Templeton Place, Earls Court. Earls Court Tube Station is a short walk from the shop.
Finish	*Go ByCycle* . Of great appeal to visitors to London as the route starts and finishes where you can rent a bike.
Distance	A 12 mile tourist bash.
Route	Starts in Earls Court and goes past the Museums and up to Hyde Park. Through the park to Marble Arch, down to Green Park to Buckingham Palace. From there to Trafalgar Square, Whitehall and past Westminster. Along the Thames into Pimlico, Chelsea and back to Earls Court.
Attractions	Takes in the sights of the National History Museum, Victoria and Albert Museum, Science Museum, Royal Albert Hall, Hyde Park, Buckingham Palace, The Mall, Trafalgar Square, Whitehall, Parliament Square, Big Ben, Embankment of River Thames, Pimlico, Chelsea and South Kensington.
Refreshments	Any number of restaurants, café's and pubs along the route. Take your pick.

(1) Turn right out of *Go ByCycle* and left to Earls Court Road. Cross with care and continue along Barkston Gardens. At the T junction go right then first left into Courtfield Gardens which you follow to Gloucester Road.

Turn right then left (2) into Stanhope Gardens across Queen's Gate to Harrington Road and South Kensington Tube Station. Bear left on the one-way system and cross busy Cromwell Road to Exhibition Road (3). On the right is the Victoria and Albert Museum. On the left is the Science Museum and Natural History Museum.

Continue up Exhibition Road to the junction with Kensington Gore. Hyde Park is to the right and Kensington Gardens to the left. Turn left onto Kensington Gore and cycle around the Royal Albert Hall on your left. Cross Kensington Gore at the Queen's Gate junction and enter the park at the cyclists' entrance.

Follow this path to the right, passing the Albert Memorial on the left. Turn left onto West Carriage Drive and cross the bridge over The Serpentine (4). Turn right onto the cycle path on the north side of The Serpentine. Pass the restaurant and turn left towards Speakers Corner at Marble Arch. Follow Park Lane south towards Hyde Park Corner, keeping to the park.

Cross over Inner Park Drive to find the entrance to the subway under the Hyde Park Corner roundabout. Descend the ramp at exit 3, follow signs for exit 6 then for 7-11 (Buckingham Palace exit). You will emerge on Constitution Hill, with Green Park on the left and Buckingham Palace Gardens to the right.

Ride along the bridlepath in Green Park to Buckingham Palace (6). Opposite the Palace is the Mall along which you proceed to Trafalgar Square. St. James's Park is to the right. Look out for the magnificent terrace to the left - Carlton House Terrace.

At Trafalgar Square is the National Portrait Gallery and Nelson's Column. Cross the top of Whitehall very carefully and turn right to go down Whitehall, passing the Cenotaph, Horse Guards Parade and Downing Street to the right (7).

At the base of Whitehall is Big Ben, Westminster Abbey and the Houses of Parliament. Exit Parliament Square at the South East corner onto Millbank. The River Thames is to the left. At Lambeth Bridge turn right to Horseferry Road and left past Westminster Hospital onto Marsham Street, leaving Westminster to enter Pimlico (8).

Take the third right onto Erasmus Street and at the end of

this street turn right, briefly onto Causton Street and left to cross Vauxhall Bridge Road (9). Pass Pimlico Tube Station and continue west along Lupus Street. Before Lupus turns left to rejoin the river side, turn right onto Sutherland Street and over the railway line south of Victoria Station at Ebury Bridge (10).

Continue straight on over Ebury Bridge onto Pimlico Road. Go straight on at the cross roads with Chelsea Bridge Road/ Lower Sloane Street to Royal Hospital Road. The National Army Museum is on the left further down Royal Hospital Road, past the home of the Chelsea Pensioners at Royal Hospital.

Take the third left after the crossroads (11) onto Franklin's Row and left at the top onto St. Leonard's Terrace. Carry on to the junction with Chelsea Manor Street and turn right onto Old Church Street. Proceed straight over Fulham Road onto Onslow Gardens, left onto Old Brompton Road and second right onto Gloucester Road (there is an excellent second-hand bookshop on the right).

Just before the major junction with Cromwell Road (2) turn left onto Courtfield Road and back to *Go ByCycle* by retracing the first part of the route.

THE LEA & THE MIMRAM

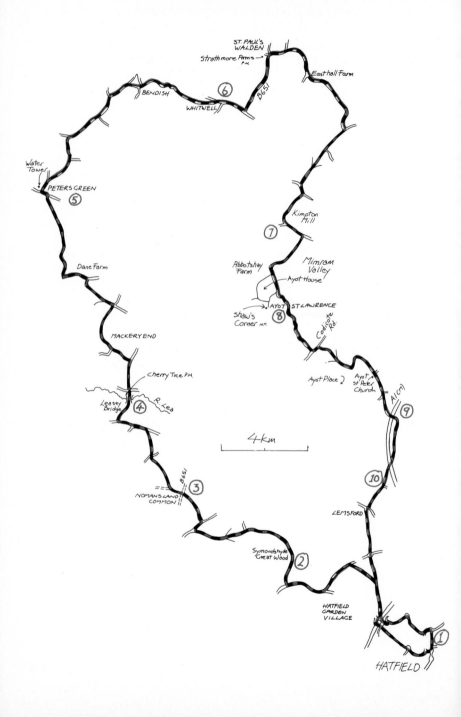

ST. PAUL'S WALDEN

Strathmore Arms P.H.

Easthall Farm

BENDISH

⑥

WHITWELL

B651

Water Tower

PETERS GREEN

⑤

Kimpton Mill

⑦

Dane Farm

Mimram Valley

Abbotshay Farm

Ayot House

MACKERY END

AYOT ST. LAWRENCE

⑧

Shaw's Corner N.T.

Codicote Rd

Cherry Tree P.H.

R. Lea

Leasey Bridge

④

Ayot Place

Ayot St. Peter Church

A1(m)

⑨

4 km

B651

⑩

③

NOMANSLAND COMMON

LEMSFORD

Symondshyde Great Wood

②

HATFIELD GARDEN VILLAGE

①

HATFIELD

THE LEA & THE MIMRAM

Map	OS LR 166 Luton and Hereford.
Start	Hatfield BR Station (trains from Kings Cross). Enquiries 0582 27612 or 071 278 2477. Car Parking at the Station.
Finish	Hatfield BR Station.
Distance	29 miles including one short section of well-drained bridleway.
Route	Once you have left Hatfield this ride is almost all on quiet winding lanes. It has many short hills, some quite steep but is sheltered from the wind and is very scenic. With an OS map you can find several bridleway 'short cuts' along the route.
Attractions	Hatfield House, Symondshyde Great Wood, Normansland Common, Whitwell, Shaw Corner.
Refreshments	Bright Star Pub - Peters Green, The Bull - Whitwell, Water Hall - Whitwell, cafés in Hatfield Town Centre.

The Great North Road, the A1, runs from London to York and Edinburgh. It was on this most important of highways that Robert Cecil built his palace, Hatfield House in 1497. When the Great Northern Railway was laid beside the road in 1848 the road became quieter than it had been since the middle ages. The motor car followed and its gradual transition from plaything to near necessity has involved the construction of a corridor much bigger and divisive than either the old highway or rail-road. The Great North Road still runs past the Gates of Hatfield House but it is now down-graded to the A1000 or the B197, while the A1M runs in a shallow tunnel a mile to the west.

The entrance to Hatfield House is directly opposite the Station (1). House and Gardens are open to the public, and there is a rather expensive tea room for visitors only. From Hatfield Station turn left at the traffic lights into St. Alban's Road East. Over the railway turn right at a small roundabout into Ground Lane. Notice the abandoned rail trackway you are crossing which used to be a branch line to St. Albans. At the next roundabout, turn left into Birchwood Avenue past the spectacular copper beech trees. Cross the roundabout and just before the big one, turn right into the service road West View. Cross the main road using the

cycle crossing on your left and go forward over the A1M to Hatfield Garden Village.

Ahead to your left is the old De Havilland Works and Airfield where the first jet air liner, The Comet, was built. Turn right along Green Lanes and after the school turn left into Great Braitch Lane. Turn left at the T junction with Coopers Green Lane. On the right leading into a field is a witty metal 'gate': the two uprights are linked with a length of wound metal cable - clearly the only trespassers expected have four wheels.

At the end of the woods turn right into Hammond Lane, signposted 'Symondshyde'. This lane runs through Symondshyde Great Wood, (2) (3 miles) open to the public with a clearing on the left for picnics and games. Descend the narrow lane to the T junction and turn right signed Colemans Green, Welwyn - then left at the sign for Wheathampstead.

Cross the B651 onto Normansland Common (3) (5 miles) and take the road up to the right signed Amwell, Down Green. The Common is administered by the Countryside Management Service (0992 555257) who promote occasional guided nature walks here and at Symondshyde Woods.

Go straight on at the staggered crossroads in the narrow lanes of Amwell, then left at the T junction onto a busier road before diving right down Leasey Bridge Lane. At the foot of this twisting overhung descent, (4) (7.5 miles) the River Lea shares the cramped valley with the track bed of another ex-branch-line. Notice the old level crossing gate almost lost in foliage. The riverside track makes a pleasant detour if you are in no hurry.

Over the river the lane rises to the B653. Cross into Marshalls Heath Lane and climb through the young oak trees which in spring have new leaves of a delicate, luminous green. Turn right into the lane signposted Mackerye End. Follow this road as it winds past Mackerye End Farm to a crossroads where you turn left into Sauncey Wood Lane, then right into Holly Lane.

At the bottom of this lane turn right into common lane and at the next T junction left along Kimpton Bottom. Although the timber barns of Dane Farm look sadly neglected, it is clearly a working farm. Turn right up the short steep Plummers lane and onto Peters Green (5) (11 miles). Keep left and then turn right past the metal water tower into Lawrence End Road. At the T junction at Wandon Green Farm turn right and follow the follow the signs for Bendish and

Whitwell. The Harrow pub in Bendish is closed, giving the village a rather forlorn look.

A long gentle descent brings you into Whitwell (6) (15 miles), a hamlet in the parish of St Paul's Walden on the banks of the river Mimram which, long ago, outgrew its hilltop neighbour. It supports three pubs and has a wealth of ancient buildings including the Brewery next to the Bull and a 17th Century village hall.

At the end of Whitwell, turn left up towards St Paul's Walden. The Water Hall Rare Breeds Farm on the left has a Tea Shop and is open from Wednesday to Sunday. The next entrance on the left is to St Paul's Walden Bury House, the seat of the Bowes-Lyon family. The formal gardens are open on some Sundays and there are occasional lakeside charity concerts. For details, enquire at the Strathmore Arms (0438 871654) at the top of the hill.

At the Strathmore turn right, keep right at the next two junctions past Easthall Farm and Rustling End to make a right turn at the T junction at Crouch Green. The hedgerows are gone from this section of lane, bad for bunnies and butterflies and leaving the poor cyclist in the wind. Turn left signed for Coldicote and right onto an unmarked road. Take care as there is a sharp lefthand bend at the bottom of the hill bringing you back to the river Mimram running directly under Kimpton Mill (7) (20 miles).

Turn left and then right up Tanyard Lane. In rainstorms this steep narrow hill becomes a watercourse as water runs off the fields on either side. At the top, the lane bends left and continues as a bridleway, with a rough but well-drained surface, past Ayot Park. It emerges through a big gateway into Ayot St. Lawrence (8) (21 miles) where the route turns left. A right turn will take you past the picturesque ruined church to the Old Rectory where George Bernard Shaw - the noted Irish motor-cyclist, vegetarian, dramatist and politician spent the second half of his life. The house is modest. G.B.S. left it to the nation.

If you have visited Shaw Corner retrace to Ayot Park gateway and carry on, bearing right to descend Hill Farm Lane. At the T junction with Codicote Road turn left and after 150 yards right up Ayot St Peter Road. Pass the Entrance to Ayot Place and Ayot St. Peter Church and on up through the fine old trees of Ayot Green to cross the A1M and rejoin the Great North Road at the top of Digswell Hill (9) (24 miles). This landmark on the old

A1 (B 197) was the starting point for 50 and 100 mile record attempts in the golden age of long distance cycling.

Turn right, the southerly line of the old road has been dug up for the motorway so to get to Lempsford turn right at the first roundabout, pass under the flyover and go straight across the next. The Long Arm and the Short Arm pub is said to refer to the wooden signal which told the coachmen whether the River Lea (10) (25 miles) was safe to ford. There is another pub on the south side of the river, long ago bridged, where northbound passengers could wait for the waters to subside. Another local legend is that the mill on the right, now converted into offices, inspired the song 'There's an old mill by the stream Nellie Dean'.

At the staggered crossroads at the entrance to Brocket Hall, cross into Green Lane and go straight on, retracing the outward route to the West View service road. Cross Birchwood Avenue, watching out for motor traffic coming fast off the roundabout, and turn left into Wellfield Road. At the roundabout in the town centre go straight on into French Horn Lane which takes you down to a final roundabout on the Great North Road. Turn left to climb a short hill to Hatfield Station (1) (29 miles).

THE RODING, THE CHELMER
THE STORT & THE CAM

LEADEN RODING

A414

M11

CHURCHGATE STREET

Mark Hall Cycle Mus.

HARLOW ⑰

⑦
Beauchamp Roding Church

Weald Lodge

MORETON

PYFIELD

⑱

A414 Cross Keys Cafe

⑤

A414 Talbot R'bout

⑥

NORTH WEALD BASSETT

④

EPPING

M11

M25

③

② Tea Shack

Epping Forest Conservation Centre

A104

A121

4 kms

①
Chingford B.R.

THE RODING, THE CHELMER
THE STORT & THE CAM

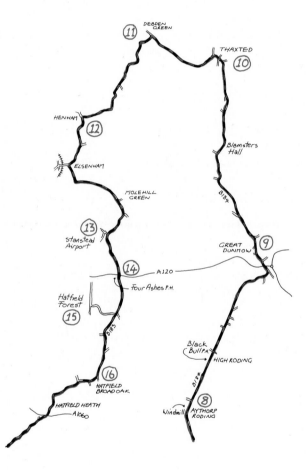

THE RODING, THE CHELMER, THE STORT & THE CAM

Map	OS LR 177 East London area. LR167 Chelmsford, Harlow and surrounding area.
Start	Chingford BR Station (trains from Liverpool Street). Car Parking here or at Connaught Water, off Rangers Road.
Finish	Chingford BR Station.
Distance	70 miles.
Route	The first leg takes you out of London through the forest to Epping. From there you ride north to Thaxted, via Great Dunmow. The return leg is parallel, a few miles to the west allowing the route to be shortened if necessary. There are no long or steep hills.
Attractions	Epping Forest, Windmills at Anythorpe Roding and Thaxted, Thaxted Guildhall and town, Hatfield Forest, Mark Hall Cycle Museum.
Refreshments	Tea shacks in Epping Forest. Tea Rooms at Beauchamp Roding. Pubs in High Roding, Dunmow and Thaxted. Cross Keys Café at Thornwood Common.

The best place to begin a cycle tour is your own front door. The second best is probably an 'end of the line' railway station which, however prosaic its surroundings, always has an air of the Frontier. Chingford Station (1) is the end of the track and quite accessible by bike from North and East London.

Turn right out of the Station and follow Rangers Road passing Queen Elizabeth's Hunting Lodge. Built in the reign of Henry VIII to allow friends of the monarch to view the hunting in comfort, it is now a museum of the History, Flora and Fauna of the Forest (081 529 6681). Over the hill you cross the Essex County Boundary and see on your left, behind a car park, Connaught Water.

Either cross the Car park to the lakeside, turn right and WALK along the path through the woods (this path opens onto Fairmead Road - turn left). or, if you want to ride, stick to the road, turn left at the T junction and 100 metres further on find the blocked entry into Fairmead Road on your left. Fairmead Road crosses the open Whitehouse Plain and then climbs into the trees.

At the end of the road is a Tea Shack (2) (2 miles) in a clearing, a popular meeting place for motor cyclists. On a summer Sunday

you may find several hundred hanging-out on the grass admiring each other's vintage or customised machines.

Turn left at the T junction and then right towards High Beach (3) (2.5 miles) where the Epping Forest Conservation Centre (081 508 7714) stands next to the Kings Oak Pub. This village is the centre of Epping Forest which has an extensive network of bridle paths to explore.

The Forest stands on a ridge between the valleys of the rivers Lea and Roding and has been wooded for more than 4,000 years. Its size over 6,000 acres - ensures you can find quietness without much trouble. It was saved from enclosure and the encroachment of 19th Century railway suburbs by the vigilance of its commoners, defending their rights to gather firewood and graze animals. It is an SSSI (Site of Special Scientific Interest), contains extensive Iron-age earthworks and as the nearest stretch of 'wilderness' to a great city, the antics of the humans who visit provide endless entertainment. It is a magnet for mountain bikers, horse riders and is generally the place where the diversity of city dwellers come to act out their fantasies of country living.

Turn right at the tea shack at the north end of High Beach

Village green. This is where the mountain bikers take refreshment. Carry on past the green, turn right at the T junction, then right when the road bends left. These forest roads are delightful. At the T junction turn right and almost immediately, at the 'City Limits' roundabout, turn left for Epping on the B1393.

The road runs straight along the ridge and through the town of Epping. Protected from London by the buffer of the Forest, Epping feels like a country town, not a suburb, but its single broad High Street with several large Inns reveals its former prosperity as a stopping place for travellers.

At the northern end of Epping, after the new Civic Centre, turn right at the lights (4) (7.5 miles) on to the B181 Ongar road. On your right is a milestone 'Epping 1, Ongar 6, London 17'. The road up from Thornwood Common joins from the left. Descend into North Weald Basset built round the perimeter of North Weald Airfield now noted mostly for giant car boot sales.

At the Talbot roundabout (5) (10.5 miles) cross the A414 and run down to Weald Bridge which crosses Cripsey Brook, a tributary of the Roding. This is the area of the villages of Magdalen, High and Little Laver. Turn right at the T junction at Weald Lodge. Essex has no stone so buildings are of brick, flint or wood. The timber barn here is the first of many big wooden buildings you will encounter. The farmhouse on the right, a mile further on, is old enough to boast a moat. Turn right at the T junction and pass through Moreton and down to meet the B184 Dunmow Road at Fyfield (6) (16 miles). Turn left.

The route now runs through a more extensive group of parishes, the eight Rodings. Beauchamp Roding Church (7) (19 miles) appears isolated in fields to your right. It is reached by a farm track and, if you feel like a rest, is a quiet spot. For those in need of more material refreshment their is a thatched tea-room a little further along the Dunmow road (0279 876343). At the A1060, turn right then left at the William IV pub in Leaden Roding to continue on the Dunmow Road.

This has always been rich corn country and Aythorpe Roding (8) (22 miles) has a white painted clapboard windmill, open on the last Sunday of each month, April to September inclusive, from 2 to 5pm (0787 269724). The next four miles of dead straight road betray Roman origins. High Roding, where the Black Bull serves food, is a one street village of thatch and timber and beyond here the road can be unpleasantly windswept, but the views across open country in all directions offer some compensation.

After the Great Dunmow town sign, turn left and climb to the town's centre (9) (28 miles). Outside the Saracens Head Hotel, turn right and pass the Starr Inn. Where the road divides, take the left fork for Thaxted. This road rolls and winds along the line of the River Chelmer. Beyond Great Easton the road drops to cross a small brook. As you climb the hill on the other side, look out for Blamsters Hall on the right with its fig tree elegantly trained on a south-facing wall. Before you see the impressive spire of Thaxted's hill top church you pass a couple of forges. This area was once Essex's armoury.

Thaxted's (10) (34 miles) half-timbered 15th Century Guildhall was built for the area's cutlers. Another landmark is John Webb's brick-built windmill, which houses a small agricultural museum (0371 830366). The steep flint paved backstreets have many houses over three hundred years old, which testify to the towns old-time prosperity based on metal working and weaving. At the Bullring, the top of the town, take the left turn signposted for Debden and Cutlers Green.

At Debden Green (11) (36 miles), turn left signposted

Henham and Stortford. This lane runs along high ground between three river systems. The Chelmer running east to Maldon on the North Sea, the Stort which joins the Lea to reach the Thames in London's East End and the Cam which runs north via the Great Ouse to the Wash at Kings Lynn.

Henham (12) (40 miles) is a grand village built round a long green. At the end of the green turn left into Crow Street signposted for Stortford. Turn right onto the B1051 and left past the jam works in Elsenham. The road skirts Stanstead Airport (13) (44 miles). Fans of modern architecture can turn right at the roundabout to admire its prize-winning terminal building, others turn left for Takeley where we cross the A120 outside the Four Ashes pub at Takeley (14) (45.5 miles).

A mile further on the B183, turn right signposted Bush End if you want to visit Hatfield Forest (15). According to Oliver Rackham in his book 'The Last Forest,' 'this is the only place (in England) where one can step back into the Middle Ages to see, with only a small effort of the imagination, what a forest looked like in use.'

On returning to the modern era, regain the B183 and follow it through Hatfield Broad Oak (16) 50 miles), named for a mighty tree that stood in the Forest until the 19th Century, and on through Hatfield Heath and Sheering to the Outskirts of Harlow.

Velophiles can carry on into the new town to visit the remarkable Mark Hall Cycle Museum (17) (57 miles) (0279 39680). Others should turn left at the roundabout and then right at the T junction. Then through one last thatch and clapboard village - Churchgate Street. This lane passes under the M11. Just before it recrosses the motorway, turn left into Mill Street and then right to come up to the giant roundabout where the A414 crosses the M11. Follow the signs for Epping.

On your left is the Cross Keys Cafe (18) (60 miles) a well known source of baked-beans for north east London's roadmen and women. If you started the tour other than at Epping, or are keen to make a second lap, a left turn at the Blacksmiths Arms in Thornwood Common takes you up to the Ongar Road. Otherwise, straight on up the long drag into Epping. Retrace the route to Chingford (70 miles).

ESSEX IS NOT FLAT -
BUCKHURST HILL, TOOT HILL, HIGH BEACH

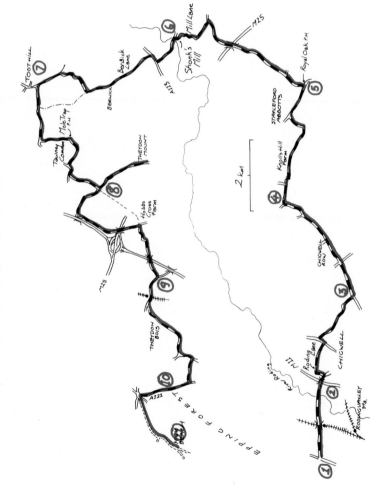

ESSEX IS NOT FLAT -
BUCKHURST HILL, TOOT HILL, HIGH BEACH

Map	OS LR 177 East London Area. LR 167 Chelmsford, Harlow and surrounding areas.
Start	Buckhurst, formerly known as Buckets-Hill is within Epping Forest. The Green on the corner of the High Road (A121) and Palmerston Road (B170) makes a pleasant rendezvous in fine weather. Get here along the A104 which in London N1 is conveniently named the Essex Road, or take the train to Chingford which is 1.5 miles to the west.
Finish	High Beach in Epping Forest. See Dunmow and Thaxted for route back to Chingford BR. The route back to Buckhurst Hill from here is also straightforward.
Distance	25 miles all on-road but there are lots of bridlepaths in the area to explore. None of the hills are high but there are lots of them.
Route	This short ride takes in the country lanes shielded from London by the undeveloped highland of Epping Forest. There are no fantastic attractions or spectacular scenery so the lanes are quiet.
Attractions	Hainault Forest, Paddling at Shonk's Mill, Hobbs Cross Farm, Epping Forest, hills.
Refreshments	The Royal Oak - Stapleford Abbots, The Mole Trap - Tawney Common, Hobbs Cross Farm.

From the junction of High Road and Palmerston Road drop down Palmerston, straight and steep, to cross the River Roding meandering across a flat bottomed valley. On the other side, turn left (2) (1.5 miles) into Roding Lane. After crossing the motorway, this becomes a tree lined climb with nice white lines in either gutter. In Chigwell, turn left and right into Vicarage Lane which is lined with some splendid oak trees.

After crossing Chigwell Brook, the lane begins to climb. In bygone days this hill had a CTC sign at the top saying 'this hill is dangerous for cyclists' but the sharp bends were long ago 'improved'. The white wooden semi-detached cottages on the first bend were originally built on top of the hill and later moved down here (an advantage of timber construction).

At the top of the hill turn left (3) (3 miles) into Lambourne Road (B173). Pass the Maypole at Chigwell Row. Hainault Forest on the right is open for the public to explore. It was a wood-pasture common equal in size to Epping Forest until the mid 19th Century when 90% of it was cut to make third rate farmland. The road climbs in rolling steps. The summit is where the road bears right (4) (5 miles) (ignore a left turn down to Abridge). Try to maintain your momentum down

the snaking descent for the short steep climb to Knolls Farm, where there are long views over the south Essex suburbs of Romford and Hornchurch.

At the T junction in Stapleford Abbots, turn right up Oak Hill Road. The Royal Oak boasts a Crab and Lobster Hut - a reminder that we are not far from the East End of London, where seafood remains plentiful and popular even if it is no longer cheap enough to be a staple.

After the Oak, turn left (5) (7.5 miles) into Tysea Hill, an unsigned residential road. The lane is quiet until it crosses the M25. The wooded ridge of Epping Forest appears in the distance to your left. Turn left into Mill Lane and descend carefully as it is narrow with some sharp bends. At the bottom is Shonk's Mill (6) (11 miles) on the River Roding. There is a little beach on the Mill Stream where paddling is recommended on hot days.

Turn left onto Shonk's Mill Road. At the T junction with the A113, London Road, turn right then left into Berwick Lane. This road climbs through woods. Pass Berwick Farm. Where the road bears right, a bridleway shortcut goes straight on and rejoins the route after Toot Hill. If you ignore it, turn left at the next T junction. At the sloping triangular village green of Toot Hill (7) (14.5 miles) keep left onto Epping Road. (The Ongar Road will take you North to join the RODING & CAM ride at Moreton). Mud-pluggers on the Berwick farm track rejoin here.

Turn left onto Tawney Common. Although the Common was long ago enclosed for agriculture, the straight unhedged road keeps a sense of open space. Turn right at the Mole Trap pub which serves food and has a lovely aspect and garden. At the T junction turn left and left again to descend through the hillside hamlet of Theydon Mount. At the bottom of the hill, the road is on the line of the same Roman Road used on the Fyfield-Dunmow Section of the RODING & CAM ride.

If you have the tyres and the time, you can go straight along the bumpy bridleway which rejoins the route at Hobbs Cross Farm. Otherwise, turn right (8) (17.5 miles) then left just before the motorway bridge. This road is new - the old lane has been cut by the M11. The lane crosses the M25 to reach Hobbs Cross Open Farm with a restaurant which in winter has a big open fire.

Turn right up Coopersale Lane past Theydon Garnon Church. At the T junction, turn right on the B172 down to Theydon Bois (9) (20.5 miles). The citizens of this village recently got so fed up with speeding cars and police inaction that they bought their own speed trap equipment. The green is expansive and luxurious at the foot of the forest.

Fork left onto the tree lined avenue of Loughton Lane. This turns into Red Oak Mead (surely this name was chosen by a developer) then becomes Debden Lane. Keep left at the triangular green, the entrance to the nicest campsite within the M25, and turn right up Clays Lane. One last steep and wooded hill. At the T junction (10) (22.5 miles) turn right and (unless you are tempted by the forest bridleways to the left) continue to the Wake Arms roundabout. Take the second exit, then immediately turn left and left again at the T junction to the woodland resort of High Beach (11) (25 miles).

OVER THE DARENT
TO DICKENS' ROCHESTER & THE MEDWAY

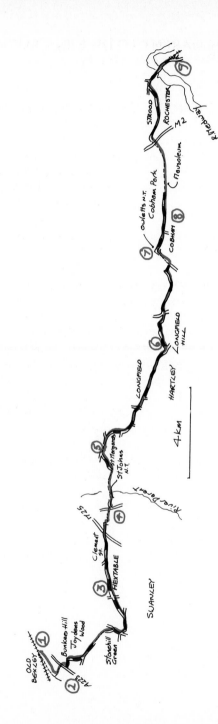

OVER THE DARENT TO DICKENS' ROCHESTER & THE MEDWAY

Map	OS LR 177 East London Area, LR 178 The Thames Estuary.
Start	Bexley Station has trains from London Bridge. It can be reached by bike from London along Watling Street (now the A207) - turn right down Upton road in Bexley Heath.
Finish	Rochester Station. Trains to Bexley and London Bridge.
Distance	20 miles with awkward off-road sections which require some walking.
Route	From the valley of the Cray, the route runs east, crossing the Darent and over wooded highland before dropping to cross the Medway into Rochester.
Attractions	Joyden's Wood, St. John's Jerusalem, Owletts, Great Wood, Rochester.
Refreshments	Leather Bottle - Cobham, lots of places in Rochester High Street.

Old Bexley is built round a crossing of the River Cray. Turn right out of the station (1) and left on Bexley High Street. Turn left into Salisbury Road and right under the railway onto Manor Way Sports Ground. Follow the footpath to your right, the Cray River Way, which can be muddy in winter. On reaching buildings, turn left down Water Lane to emerge by Loring Hall (2) (1.5 miles), now a nursing home but once a politician's country house.

Bexley's proximity to London and Watling Street meant it was a desirable place for the wealthy to live before it became engulfed by suburbia. The busy and unattractive A223 presents a barrier.

The route goes up Bunkers Hill, a muddy lane about three hundred yards to the right. Bunkers Hill climbs out of Greater London and into Kent. The safest way into it is to turn right in front of Loring Hall and use the pavement before crossing the dual carriageway. Bunkers Hill bears right and becomes Cocksure Lane.

Turn left at the 'T' and follow the deteriorating path - it can be very slimy - into Joyden's Wood. The wood contains Faestens Dic, an old earthwork that probably marked the limit of the Saxon Kingdom of Kent. The sign says you need a licence to ride a horse here; bikes are not mentioned. If you can ride, go slowly with care and give way to walkers and horses. Go straight on over the hill. On a clear day you can see across 12 miles to the towers of central London. The path emerges into Kent by two conical Oast houses - built to dry hops - but here the gardens have been replaced by a golf range.

Turn right onto Stonehill Green Road, right into Birchwood Road and left into Ladenhatch Lane. Fork left into College Road. Ahead are woods, fields and villages all the way to the Medway. Go straight on at the village green (3) (4.5 miles) in Hextable into Lower Road which becomes Clement Street and leads through a straggling hamlet of the same name.

Just across the M25, turn right into Church Road and descend into the Darent Valley. Turn right onto the A225 then immediately left (4) (7 miles) into Tallents Close. Follow this track down and continue on a footpath. On the right is St. John's Jerusalem, built by the Knights Templars in the middle ages. This order of armed men was formed to protect Christian pilgrims who set off to visit Palestine following the capture of Jerusalem in 1099. It has been a private house for centuries, but the gardens and chapel are open to the public.

Across the river was the site of a Roman Villa.

On reaching the tarmac bank turn right on Roman Villa Road. Take the next left (carry straight on if you want to join the PILGRIMS WAY route at Farningham) onto a farm track and follow it to St. Margarets. Turn left over the hill through the orchards and down to Green Street Road (B260) (5) (9.5 miles). Turn right onto the B260 and follow it through Longfield and up to Longfield Hill. Turn left (6) (12.5 miles) by the village hall along a switch-back road past Nurstead Court and on along White Posts Lane to Sole Street.

Turn right (7) (14.5 miles) at the T junction and left at the next one. Turn right outside Owletts, a seventeenth century brick house owned by the National Trust. Turn right into Cobham where St. Marys Church has a famous collection of brass memorials.

The Leather Bottle claims to have been a favoured haunt of Charles Dickens, who put it in the Pickwick Papers. The sign on the leather bottle is early warning that you are nearing Rochester where Dickens-mania rules. Keep straight on at the metal gate (8) (16 miles) and follow the track across open ground into the woods. On the map, this track is marked as a footpath, but clearly

sees a lot of four-wheeled vehicles driven by joy-riders who have left several burnt-out shells along the way. This and the giant derelict Mausoleum at the top of the hill give it a very mysterious air. Beyond the Mausoleum the going improves as the track descends to the M2 embankment.

Turn left to find the underpass leading into Albatross Avenue. Turn right into Bligh Way then left onto the A228 which leads through Strood across the Medway into Rochester. On the bridge, get into the righthand lane marked 'ESP' for esplanade. On the far side, cross into the pedestrianised High Street (9) (20 miles) which is full of tea shops and cafés - including one called a 'Taste of two Cities'. Dickens liked Rochester, and the city certainly returns the compliment. Every second building on the narrow, well-preserved high street - we are on Watling Street - claims a connection to the fellow.

The Dickens Centre in Eastgate (0634 844176) is lively and popular. There is a quirky motorcycle museum behind the shop at 144, High Street and the Guildhall Museum, also in the High Street is strong on the history of sailing barges on the Medway.

THE PILGRIMS WAY

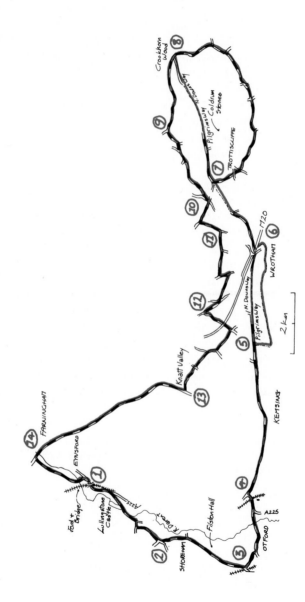

THE PILGRIMS WAY

Map | OS LR 188 Maidstone and the Weald of Kent covers almost all the route. The northernmost two miles are on LR 177 East London area.

Start | Eynsford Station. London trains from Victoria or Kings Cross (Thameslink) not Sundays. More trains stop at Otford on Sunday so this could be used as an alternative starting point.

Finish | Eynsford Station.

Distance | 30.5 miles with 4 miles of off-road stretches on The Pilgrims Way. It can be muddy in wet weather and is often narrow, so consideration must be given to pedestrians and horse riders.

Route | The route follows the Darent Valley south and turns east on the Pilgrims Way along the foot of the North Downs but at sufficient height to give wide views to the south. A long steep climb takes the route to the top of the Downs. Quiet lanes take us west to begin a long roll back down to the Darent.

Attractions | Lullingstone House and Park. The villages of Shoreham and Wrotham. Coldrum Stones. The Pilgrims Way and the North Downs.

Refreshments | Lullingstone Castle, Pubs in Wrotham.

In prehistoric times crossing the Straits of Dover was a hit and miss affair and landfall could be made anywhere along the coast, from Folkestone to Ramsgate. An inland centre, on high ground, equally convenient for all these landings grew up in the area of Canterbury. The high ground of Salisbury Plain was the main centre of population in prehistoric Southern England. Long before the Christian Saints, Swithun of Winchester and Thomas of Canterbury made the road into a path of pilgrimage, a trade route between the two areas grew up. Over the centuries the feet of countless humans and animals made this into a well trodden track.

Leaving Eynsford Station (1) turn left onto the A225 under the railway bridge. On the right is Lullingstone Castle, one of many old buildings, ruins and archaeological sites along the Darent Valley. The gateway built in 1497 is one of the earliest brick gatehouses in England. The little church of St Botolph's is Norman and the house Tudor although the exterior was completely remodelled in the 18th Century when modernity had more status than antiquity and planning regulations were less strict. The three face each other across a wide lawn.

The church contains a macabre collection of tombs and lots of 18th century furnishings. The house is open in the afternoons on weekends and Bank Holidays, April to September and teas are served in the gatehouse (Information 0322 862114). Follow the signs for Lullington Park Visitors Centre. The grounds of the Castle are now run by Sevenoaks District Council with signed walks in woods and open country, a visitor centre, cafeteria and bookshop.

Turn left on the hill, after passing a ruined castle over the river on the left, and then fork left (2) (2 miles) following signs to Shoreham. If you want to visit the village turn left down towards the River Darent. There is a an exhibition on local wildlife at the railway station and also a little museum of World War II aircraft relics. Continue on (or regain) the High Street and continue south past Filston Hall.

Just before the railway turn left (3) (4.5 miles) into Twitton Lane. Continue past the Rising Sun at Twitton, left at the T junction joining the line of the Pilgrim's Way and on to Otford. Go straight on at the roundabout by the village pond. The Willow Tea Rooms are on the left. Cross the railway and pass the station, turn right (4) (6 miles) into the Pilgrims Way East. Continue along this road with the scarp slope of the Downs on your left and Kemsing village on your right.

Beyond Kemsing you can see a parallel route running about halfway between the Pilgrims Way and the M26. Where the road swings right (5) (9.5 miles), if you do not want to ride the trackway, go down to this parallel lane and follow it to rejoin the route in Wrotham. Otherwise keep straight on the track signed North Downs Way, crossing over a lane coming down the hill, to reach tarmac above Wrotham. The main street in Wrotham opens into a small square in front of the church, which has a passageway cut through its tower. On the Hotel a plaque recalls a shooting in the Napoleonic Wars.

If you do not want to explore the village hold the line of the Pilgrims Way over the crossroads. Turn left onto the tarmac bridleway, then left onto the A227 to cross the M20 and then take the third exit from the roundabout (6) (11.5 miles) to rejoin the line of the Way. When the road bends sharp right, continue straight on to the track and veer right on the lower path along the foot of the Downs. Turn right when you reach the metalled road.

Trottiscliffe (pronounced Trosley) is reached by forking right (7) (13.5 miles). Trottiscliffe church contains a curiosity, a pulpit salvaged from Westminster Abbey in 1820, when it got in the way during preparations for the coronation of George IV. In its present context it appears very oversized. More impressive are the Coldrum Stones a very well preserved neolithic Long Barrow a little further along the valley. Drop down to Trottiscliffe if you want to look at the church, find the stones or avoid the final and longest section of off-road riding. Otherwise fork left following the Pilgrims Way above the village into Trosley Country Park. Carry on past the seats to the narrow track and then fork left.

On reaching the metalled road (8) (16 miles) and, having crept along at their feet for ten miles prepare to scale the North Downs. Keep left (9) (18 miles) at the top of this long, and in places steep climb, following signs for Vigo village. Turn left at the T junction and right at the Vigo Inn (10) (19.5 miles) and continue to Fairseat.

Turn left at the sign for Wrotham and Borough Green. Turn right (11) (20.5 miles) at the signpost Labour in Vain, then left at the T junction signed for Wrotham and Borough Green. Turn left and right onto the A20 signposted West Kingsdown. Take the next left (12) (23 miles) into Terrys Lodge Road and pass under the M20. Turn right at the crossroads then right and left to descend the steep Knatts Valley.

Turn right at the T junction (13) (25.5 miles) and enjoy a long gentle descent to Farningham. Turn right and left into Farningham High Street. Notice the weird two dimensional bridge downstream as you cross the river Darent. Climbing the High Street across the river turn left (14) (29 miles) by the barber shop into Sparepenny lane. At the T junction turn left (a right turn will take you to the site of a Roman Villa) along Riverside to cross the Darent by ford or bridge. Eynsford Castle was built by Normans about 900 years ago. Most of its outer walls are still standing. Turn right on the A225 to return to the Station (1) (30.5 miles).

GREENSAND RIDGE WEST - CHARTWELL, WESTERHAM & THE PATHS OF GLORY

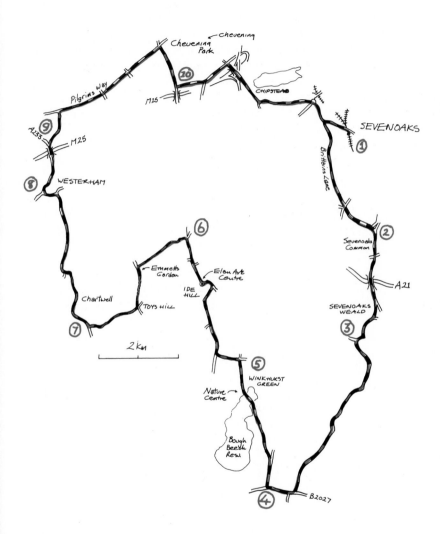

GREENSAND RIDGE WEST - CHARTWELL, WESTERHAM & THE PATHS OF GLORY

Map	OS LR 188 Maidstone and the Weald of Kent covers almost all the route except for Westerham which is on LR 187 Dorking, Reigate and Crawley.
Start	Sevenoaks BR Station. London trains from Charing Cross, Waterloo East, Victoria (not very good on Sundays) or Kings Cross (Thameslink) not Sundays.
Finish	Sevenoaks BR Station.
Distance	25 miles all on roads with several big hills.
Route	The route crosses the Greensand Ridge, descends onto the Low Weald and regains the wooded heights of Ide and Toys Hills. It returns to Sevenoaks via Westerham and a short metalled section of the Pilgrims Way.
Attractions	Bough Beech, Emmetts Gardens, Toys Hill, Chartwell and Westerham.
Refreshments	Sevenoaks, Westerham.

Sevenoaks stands on the Greensand Ridge which runs east to west across the Weald of Kent. The hills of this ridge are well wooded although many trees were blown down in the great storm of 1987, in which Sevenoaks became 'one oak.' The Cafe in Sevenoaks Cattle Market is open on Sunday Mornings.

Leave the Station (1) and turn left onto the A224. Run downhill and on top of a small rise turn left into Brittains Lane. This is a long climb. Go straight on at the crossroads signposted for Weald and Tonbridge.

Turn right at the T junction (2) (2.5 miles) and straight on at the crossroads, descending from the heights of Sevenoaks Common across the Sevenoaks bypass. Fork right at the Church and continue into Sevenoaks Weald. Turn right at the T junction by the Windmill Pub. Turn left (3) (4.5 miles) at the signpost for Chiddingstone and go down a delightful twisting lane. Turn right at the T junction onto the B2027.

Turn right (4) (7.5 miles) at the sign post for Ide Hill. (This is the valley of the Eden and if you stay on the B2027 you will connect with the EDEN VALE TO HIGH ROCKS ride). Climbing steadily upwards turn left at the signpost for Winkhurst Green to cross the Bough Beech Reservoir which was opened in 1969.

The reservoir is filled in winter and empties in summer. Areas of Kent are quite short of water and the problems of finding enough fresh water to mix concrete is one of the lesser known reasons for the delay of the Channel Tunnel. The reservoir is an important site for waterbirds and the Kent Trust for Nature Conservation has converted an Oast house into a visitors centre (5) (9.5 miles) with exhibitions of local history and wildlife. It is open April to October, at weekends and on Wednesdays. You get a good view of the reserve from the road but access is by permit only.

Turn right at the T junction on the B2042 signed for Ide Hill. This long steady climb takes you back onto the Sevenoaks ridge. At the top you can catch your breath, look back and admire the view across Bough Beech and the Low Weald. Go straight on then left into the village. There are teas at the Elan Arts Centre and pubs in the village. Turn right at the roundabout and continue until the signpost for Toys Hill points to the left (6) (12.5 miles).

The entrance to Emmetts Garden is here. The gardens contain rare specimen trees and shrubs and the high sloping site gives fine views across the Weald. (Information 0892

890651). There is also a café. Turn left and begin the climb of Toys Hill, one of the highest in Kent.

The woods here were devastated in the gale of 1987 and in places the National Trust declared a non-intervention zone so the way in which the wood repairs itself could be studied. Woods have always been a feature of Kent - it has more ancient woodland than any other county in Britain. Six years on, the only obvious evidence of the great storm are the open spaces on the exposed ridges where the lost trees have been replaced with new vistas.

At the T junction turn left and continue past the Fox and Hounds pub to descend the steep hill. Turn right past the memorial, where the views are magnificent, down the steep and narrow lane. Turn right (7) (15.5 miles) up another long hill past Chartwell. This was the home of Winston Churchill from 1922 until his death in 1964. A group of his close friends bought the house and park in 1954 to give to the National Trust. Churchill spent many years in middle-age out of office and as well as writing history he practised his brick-laying skills constructing walls in the gardens (information 0732 866368).

Turn right at the T junction onto the B2026 and after a short climb enjoy the long descent into Westerham. Turn left onto the A25 to ride into Westerham (8) (17.5 miles).

This charming westernmost town in Kent, is celebrated for its famous citizens. William Pitt joins Churchill as a local Prime Minister. Pitts Cottage Restaurant is on the A25 West of the Town but it is James Wolfe who is Westerham's favourite son. The Town Square and his boyhood home which stands at the corner of the Edenbridge and Sevenoaks Roads were renamed 'Quebec' after his conquest. Wolfe's audacity on the St. Lawrence River in 1759 certainly changed the course of history. His death in the hour of victory and his modesty - he is reputed to have said he would rather have written Gray's Elegy than take Quebec - contributed to his cult. It is also said that 'he studied heroism as a craft'. Quebec House is open to the public (information 0959 62206) and contains an exhibition of his famous victory.

Squerryes Court off the A25 west of the town is also open to the public (0959 62345). This is a 17th Century House built in brick with portraits and a monument to Wolfe. Turn right after the green, with its statue of Churchill, onto the A233 for Bromley. After crossing the M25 turn right (9) (18 miles) into a small lane and right at the T junction onto the Pilgrims Way. Follow the Way turning right and left at a staggered crossroads. Turn off the Way at a T junction, round a sharp lefthand bend (10) (21.5 miles) and left at the next T junction onto the B 221 signed for Chipstead.

Turn right at the crossroads for Chipstead and Sevenoaks over the Motorway junction. In Chipstead High Street turn left, following the signs for Rivermead and Sevenoaks. Continue over the crossroads by the telephone box. Turn left onto the A25 and at the roundabout (11) (24 miles) right up Amherst Hill the A224 towards Sevenoaks. Cross the railway and turn left into Sevenoaks Station (1) (25 miles).

GREENSAND RIDGE EAST - ORCHARDS AND WOODS

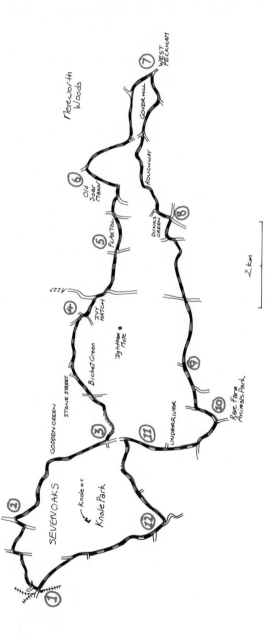

GREENSAND RIDGE EAST -
ORCHARDS AND WOODS

Map	OS LR 188 Maidstone and the Weald of Kent.
Start	Sevenoaks Station. London trains from Charing Cross, Waterloo East, Victoria (not very good on Sundays) or Kings Cross (Thameslink) not Sundays.
Finish	Sevenoaks Station.
Distance	23 miles all on roads with some big hills.
Route	The route climbs the Greensand Ridge and follows it to Ivy Hatch and Mereworth Woods, it descends to West Peckham and takes a lower route back before the final killer climb from Underriver.
Attractions	Ightham Mote, Old Soar Manor, Mereworth Woods, West Peckham, Hollanden Rare Breeds Farm, Knole Park.
Refreshments	Sevenoaks, The Sun Inn - West Peckham.

From Sevenoaks Railway Station (1), turn left onto the main road by the Railway and Bicycle Pub. The sign depicts the most civilised form of long distance door to door travel, which seems sadly to be in decline due to political dogma. Turn immediately right into Hitchen Hatch Lane past the cattle market where there is a cafe open on Sunday mornings. Go straight on at the cross roads up Mount Harry Road to the A225. Turn left at the T junction and continue past the United Reform Church. Turn right into Quakers Hall Lane by the Parish Church of St. John and left at the T junction onto the B2019.

Turn right (2) (1.5 miles) by the telephone box following the sign for Godden Green then right at the T junction close to the Buck's Head in Godden Green. Turn left at the crossroads (3) (3.5 miles) signposted Stone Street. You have climbed the Greensand Ridge and will now follow it east to Ivy Hatch. Turn right at the T junction by the Rose and Crown in Stone Street. If you want to visit Ightham Mote (information 0732 810378) turn right (4) (6 miles) just past the sign for Ivy Hatch.

This mediaeval moated manor house has some later additions but its remote valley setting helps to give a feeling of the life of aristocrats and their households in the 14th Century. The great hall; the solar - a living room on the top floor - and the chapel are all open for inspection. If you cannot face the steep climb back to Ivy Hatch you can carry on down to rejoin the route on its way back to Sevenoaks. Otherwise you can visit the house later on the route.

Carry on into Ivy Hatch and turn right by the Plough, signposted for Plaxtol and Shipbourne. This begins the descent from the Greensand Ridge. Turn right onto the A227 and fork left on the hill signed for Plaxtol. In Plaxtol Village keep right after the church and turn left (5) (7 miles) at the Rorty Crankle Inn. 'Rorty Crankle' is Anglo Saxon for happy place.

Turn second right after the telephone box at the sign for Old Soar Manor (information 0732 810622). The house (6) (8.5 miles) shares many features with Ightham but is a hundred years older. Entrance is free. There is an exhibition which deals with local history as well as the owners of the house. The narrow lane on which Old Soar Manor stands climbs back up the ridge giving views over the orchards to Plaxtol.

Turn right at the T junction. Mereworth Woods, to the left, contain several good bridlepaths. Kent's coppiced woodlands were used to supply poles for the hop gardens and later, when wire replaced wood in the high frames on which the plants were trained, for fencing. Turn right at the T junction and descend the steep hill. Turn left then right into West Peckham.

The village green (7) (11 miles) is a good spot to rest on a summer day. The Church of St. Dunstan has a giant family pew, with its own exclusive entrance and exit so the occupants did not have to mingle with their inferiors. It also has a double splayed window at the base of the tower. For those less interested in church architecture the Sun Inn stands across the Green. Leave the village by the same road you entered on this time forking left signposted Plaxtol and Borough Green. On Gover Hill there are fine views to the South over the Medway to the High Weald.

Continue straight on through Gover Hill then turn left down Roughway Lane. Turn left by the Kentish Rifleman at Dunks Green, signed for Shipbourne and Tonbridge. Turn right at the crossroads (8) (14 miles). Fork left by the row of cottages, and cross the A277 into the lane signed for Hildenborough. Take the next lane up to the right (9) (16.5 miles) if you want to visit Ightham Mote, or if you are

coming down from there, rejoin the route here.

Turn left at the T junction then right (10) (17.5 miles) at the next one following signs for Underriver. A left turn here will take you the Hollanden Rare Breeds Farm (0732 832276). Here there are sixty breeds of cattle, sheep, pigs and goats not normally found on modern working farms. There is also a tea shop. Fork right and continue through Underriver. It has a river and it is under a big hill, which must be climbed to get back to Sevenoaks. After the top of the long steep hill turn left (11) (19.5 miles) signposted for Riverhill and Sevenoaks. Turn left at the T junction and continue, with Knole Park on your right, to River Hill. Turn right up the A225.

If you want to connect with the GREENSAND RIDGE WEST ride turn left (12) (21 miles) on top of the hill at the sign post for Ide Hill. Otherwise scorch down the A225 into Sevenoaks forking left onto the A224 by the Midland Bank and take the road to the station (1) (23 miles) by the Railway and Bicycle Pub.

If you have time you can visit Knole, one of the largest private houses in England, standing above the town in a wooded Deer Park.

DOWN TO RYE & ROMNEY MARSH

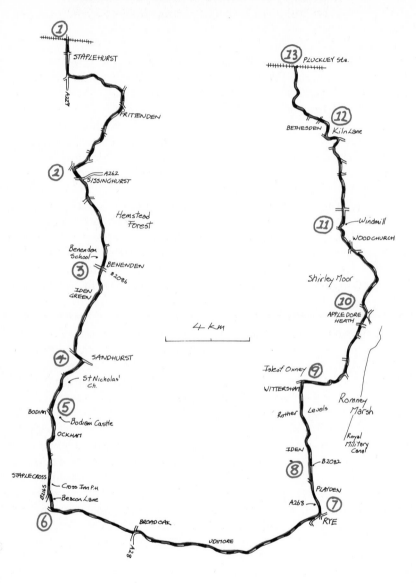

DOWN TO RYE & ROMNEY MARSH

Map	OS LR 188 Maidstone and the Weald of Kent, LR 189 Ashford and Romney Marsh and a very short distance on LR199 Eastbourne, Hastings and surrounding area.
Start	Staplehurst BR Station. One hour from London, Charing Cross on the BT1 (Boat Train) line. There is a large station car park.
Finish	Pluckley BR Station with trains to Charing Cross and Staplehurst. Pluckley is an easy 10 miles from Staplehurst if you want to make the ride circular.
Distance	47 miles, all on road with some moderate hills and extended flat sections.
Route	The route is a horseshoe running south across the Weald into Sussex, turning east behind Hastings before dropping to Rye. It skirts Romney Marsh as it returns north in a direct line to regain the railway at Pluckley on the North Downs.
Attractions	Sissinghurst Gardens, Bodiam Castle, Rye, Woodchurch Windmill, long views across the coast.
Refreshments	Pubs in many villages. Untold tea shops in Rye.

Leave the station (1) with the car-park on your left. On reaching the A229, turn left and follow it south through the village. After the church, turn left signposted for Frittenden. At the T junction turn right and pass through Frittenden, the first of many picturesque villages. At the next T junction, turn left (2) (7 miles), then left again at the A262. The route continues south by turning right opposite the Bull Inn. If you want to visit Sissinghurst Gardens, the entrance is on the left off the A262 just beyond the village.

The Garden (0580 712850) is open every day except Monday - you can visit the lush meadows that surround it free of charge. The Gardens were designed by Vita Sackville West who moved here from the Knowle in Sevenoaks in 1930, and are now owned by the National Trust. It is pleasant to rest in gardens built by the passion of others but when did they ever find time to ride their bikes?

South from the Bull go straight over the crossroads following signs for Beneden and Sandhurst. Go straight on (3) (10.5 miles) at the crossroads with the B2086. The road rolls south through fine scenery. At the A268, turn left into Sandhurst and right (4) (13.5 miles) onto the hilly road to Bodiam. A turn to the left takes you to St Nicholas' - a mediaeval church set on a hillside with fine views. The road drops to cross Kent Ditch, a side stream of the River Rother and the Kent/Sussex border. On the next hill Bodiam Church has stood since the 13th century and from its hilltop overlooks the impressive remains of Bodiam Castle.

Descend to the Castle (5) (16 miles), another National Trust property (information 058 083 436). It was built at the peak of castle building technology, with moat, drawbridge and portcullis, one of the last true castles built in England. It was built for defence, not just to advertise the status of its owner, during a European invasion scare in 1387. It guards the formerly navigable River Rother where it leaves the coastal plain.

Pass the castle and climb to Staplecross. At the Cross Inn go straight on, on the B2165. Take the first left, Beacon Lane. At the T junction (6) (19 miles) turn left onto the B2099 which descends gently in steps all the way down the ridge to Rye (7) (27.5 miles). This is one of the best preserved towns in Sussex with narrow cobbled streets. It mostly dates from the 16th century. Before that it was burnt once or twice by the French.

When you are ready to leave the bustling town, find the A268 for London - it leaves the town by an ancient gate. Follow this north through Playden then take the B2082 left (8) (29 miles) signposted Iden and Tenterden. Follow the B2082 through Iden towards Wittersham. The road drops to re-enter Kent on the Rother Levels, then climbs onto the Isle of Oxney, whose name predates the draining of the marshes. Turn right (9) (32.5 miles) by the windmill and follow the road to Stone in Oxney.

All along this road there are views east across the mysterious polders of Romney Marsh. Its limit is marked by the Royal Military Canal, dug in 1803 as a barrier against revolutionary France. It was planned to provide free movement of munitions and allowed the construction of a artillery emplacements every 1/4 mile. The idea was to flood the Marsh in the event of a French landing. Reinforcing the idea of the Marsh, with its history of smuggling, as another country.

Pass through Stone at Oxney. At the crossroads with the B2080

go straight on and at the next crossroads go left (10) (36.5 miles) towards Woodchurch. In Woodchurch, turn right at the Stonebridge Inn. Pass the village green and follow the road to the right towards Bethersden. As you leave the village you pass a big white windmill (11) (40 miles) on your right. This is the survivor of a pair of twins and was restored during the 1970's and 80's it contains an exhibition of photographs and machinery (information 023386 519).

At the T junction with the A28 turn left, then first right into Kiln Lane; At the end of this lane turn left (12) (43.5 miles), and follow this road to Pluckley. The Station (13) (47 miles) is on your right as you cross the railway bridge. The village is two miles further on. Drinkers can choose the pub by the Station or the livelier Black Horse in the village. Pluckley was promoted as the most haunted village in England during the 1970's and is now famed as the setting for H.E. Bates 'The Darling Buds of May' and its popular TV spin- off.

EDEN VALE AND HIGH ROCKS

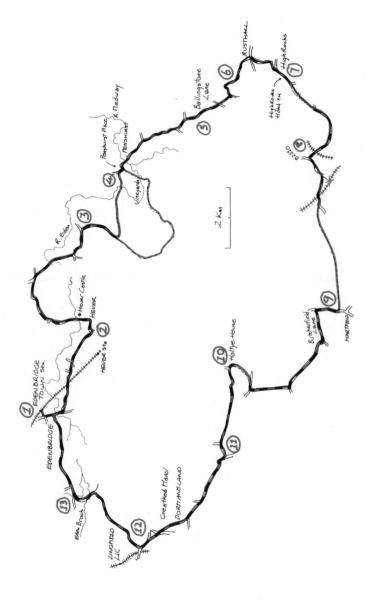

EDEN VALE AND HIGH ROCKS

Map	OS LR 188 Maidstone and the Weald of Kent and 187 Dorking, Reigate and Crawley area.
Start	Edenbridge Town BR Station. Trains from Redhill and Tonbridge or from Victoria, change at Redhill. On Sundays an alternative is to use the Station at Hurst Green with direct trains to Victoria and to cycle from there to Edenbridge (about 5 miles on lanes).
Finish	Same as the start.
Distance	34 miles with one notable climb to Rusthall. Two gentle off-road sections which could be by-passed if conditions are very wet.
Route	The route follows the River Eden to its junction with the Medway, then climbs onto the Sandstone ridge of the High Weald then returns by a more remote route to Edenbridge.
Attractions	Hever Castle, Chiddingstone, Penshurst, High Rocks, the Forest Way and Haxted Mill.
Refreshments	Tea Rooms at Chiddingstone. The High Rocks Hotel. Haxted Mill.

From Edenbridge station (1) turn left at the T junction into town. There is a cafe down the road opposite the bank but it is not open on Sundays. Continue down the High Street and take the first left after the bridge, signposted for Hever and Chiddingstone.

In Hever turn left (2) (2.5 miles) by the bus shelter and follow the road left round the King Henry VIII pub. On the right is the entrance to Hever Castle, built in the 13th Century and restored by William Waldorf Astor in 1906. He had the surrounding 'Tudor village' built as accommodation for his guests. A thousand workers were employed on the building and the creation of the huge Italian Gardens. This was the childhood home of Anne Boleyn (information 0732 865224).

Continue onto the B2027 by the Wheatsheaf pub. (You can easily link with the WEST GREENSAND RIDGE ride from here.) Turn right after the garage, at the signpost for Chiddingstone and cross the river Eden for a third time. Ahead is Chiddingstone castle. The house is in late 18th Century gothic revival style and rather outshone by its grander neighbour. It does however boast the largest display of Japanese lacquer outside Japan and has an unusual collection of Jacobite relics. Turn left and continue through Chiddingstone High Street which is owned in its entirety by the National Trust and much in demand as a period location for films. The Village Stores date from 1453.

Keep right at the converted oast houses (3) (7 miles) and continue through Wellers Town. Turn left onto a bridleway through the woods to make another crossing of the Eden. Pass through the gate and cross the field to the next gate. Turn left onto the track and keep left through the farm buildings. Turn left onto the metalled drive.

Reach the road (4) (9 miles) and turn right into Penshurst. Turn right at the T junction if you want to visit the vineyard or the Off-Road Cycling Circuit in Viceroy's Wood. Viceroy's Wood is a space dedicated to off-road bike racing and riding and its operator, Mike Westphal, hopes to build changing rooms showers and a clubhouse. To find it ride through the village and turn right after crossing the bridge. There is racing every Sunday in summer and on Wednesday nights. In the winter there is a race every month. At other times the woods are open to any visiting fun riders (information 0892 870136). If you have been to see Mike and his wood retrace to the T junction.

If you don't want the race circuit or the vineyard turn left at the T junction onto the B2176 signed for Southborough. Notice the group of half-timbered houses forming an inhabited lych gate at the entrance to the churchyard opposite the Leicester Arms Hotel. On the left is the entrance to Penshurst Place, a mediaeval house with magnificent gardens and other attractions including a toy and farm museum and adventure playground. Cross the River. This is now the Medway and the Eden joins it just above the bridge.

Climb the steep hill past Swaylands School. Turn right, signed for Spelhurst and keep left at the half-timbered house. Turn right (5) (11 miles) into Ballingstone Lane, which is beautiful and in places steep. Turn right at the T junction and immediately left down Burnt House Lane. Turn left at the T junction signposted Rusthall, for more climbing round the sharp bend to reach the village.

The lanes since the Medway have brought us up onto the High Weald, a forested ridge which stretches eastwards from Horsham and is bordered to the north, east and south by the clay valleys of the Low Weald. The road continues into Rusthall High Street, (6) (13 miles). Turn right at the crossroads on the common, signposted Rusthall

Church, then right and left across the A264 to go down Tea Garden Lane. Pass the Beacon Pub and glide down to the T junction. Turn right and cross the abandoned railway and the Sussex County boundary.

On your left is High Rocks (7) (14.5 miles) which together with nearby Harrison's Rocks are the only natural rock outcrops in South East England. They are a mecca for climbers. The soft sandstone suffered considerable erosion in the era of nailed boots and now climbing on them is forbidden in anything but soft shoes. Julie Tullis is probably the most illustrious mountaineer associated with the area. The rocks are fenced if you want to explore them closely purchase a ticket from the High Rocks Hotel Pub.

Continue past the pub and turn right at the T junction to reach Groombridge. This village straddles the Kent/Sussex Border and the prettiest part is reached by turning right onto the B2110. Turn left (8) (17 miles) onto the B2110 and follow it round to the right at the junction with the B2188. Cross the railway and continue to the disused rail embankment. In pre-Beeching days a rail service used to connect Tunbridge Wells with East Grinstead. Go through the gate on the other side of the embankment and climb the shallow steps. Continue along the old trackbed crossing a road to reach the old Hartfield Station.

If you want to visit the village pub turn left, otherwise go right (9) (21 miles) onto the B2026, then turn left into Butcherfield Lane. Butcherfield leads into Cansiron Lane and together they make excellent riding, climbing in steps. Cross the A264 into the lane signposted Cowden, Narrow Road. Turn left at the T junction and left (10) (25 miles) at the bottom of the hill. Follow this lane past Furnace Pond - a hammer Pond.

This lane, following the stream and the Sussex/Kent border, is overhung with trees and is truly delightful. Turn right (11) (27 miles) at the T junction and continue into Dormansland. Follow the sign for Lingfield across the crossroads. Turn left at the junction with the B2028.

Turn right (12) (30 miles) before the railway bridge, through the grounds of St. Piers School. Turn left at the T junction to greet the young River Eden. Turn right (13) (32.5 miles) at the next T junction signed for Haxted and Edenbridge. The Mill at Haxted is a museum and restaurant and well worth a visit. Turn left and then right in Edenbridge to return to the Station (1) (35 miles).

ASHDOWN FOREST & THE BLUEBELL RAILWAY

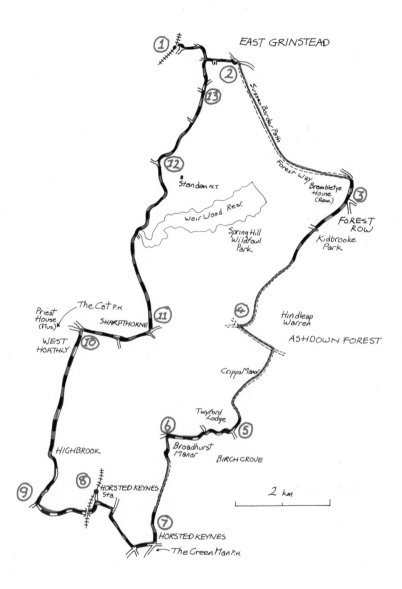

ASHDOWN FOREST & THE BLUEBELL RAILWAY

Map	OS LR 187 Dorking, Reigate & Crawley.
Start	East Grinstead Railway Station. Car Parking available.
Finish	Same as the start.
Distance	17 miles of road and 3 miles (in two sections) off-road.
Route	A circular route south of East Grinstead incorporating narrow country lanes and two stretches of the Sussex border path - one of 2 miles and one of 1 mile. It goes through Ashdown forest to Horsted Keynes, the Bluebell Railway, Sharpthorne, the Weir Wood reservoir and back to East Grinstead. The off-road sections are flat. there are a few climbs, one particularly steep. The rest of the route is best described as undulating with the downhill stretches and glorious country lanes making up for the uphill sections.
Attractions	Ashdown Forest, Horsted Keynes, Bluebell Railway, West Hoathly, Standen NT.
Refreshments	The Green Man - Horsted Keynes, The Cat - West Hoathly, Vinols Cross Inn - Sharpthorne.

(1) Turn left out of the station and move carefully to the right hand side of the one-way system. Keep right at the T junction and pass over the A22 main road underpass to proceed along London Road the short distance to the centre of East Grinstead. Go past the shops to the mini roundabout and turn left onto the wide High Street.

East Grinstead had many old buildings of architectural note, particularly the terrace of timbered properties on the right off the High Street. Carry on through the High Street and pause at the best building of all on your left just before the roundabout junction with the A22. Here is the magnificent Sackville College, open to the public from May to September.

Just before the roundabout, cross to the right-hand side of the road and find the access point for the Forest Way path 20 yards past the roundabout (2). Join the path and give way to pedestrians on the first narrow section of 100 yards. Cross Herontye Road where you will be on a wider section of the old railway line from East Grinstead to Forest Row. It is signposted as Forest Way country park.

Continue on the track for almost two miles to cross the A22 at Forest Row, where the track comes alongside a stream.

Brambletye Manor Farm (remains of Brambletye House) is to the right (3). Turn right here for a very short section on the main road through Forest Row. Turn right at the mini-roundabout just after the traffic lights, in front of the imposing church spire. This is Priory Road.

The road goes uphill past the Rudolph Steiner School to the left and the Weir Wood fly fishery to the right. The road runs through the edge of Ashdown Forest with Kidbrooke Park to the left and Spring Hill Wildfowl Park to the right. (4) Turn left at the crossroads, two miles from Forest Row, signposted for Wych Cross. The entrance to Cripps Manor is to the right.

Continue on this road for half a mile with the aptly named Hindleap Warren on the left. Ashdown Forest is known for its deer as well as for A A Milne, who lived and wrote his Winnie the Pooh stories nearby. Turn right on a very narrow lane signposted for Twyford. This is a very pleasant run through fern clad mixed woodland with ancient beeches visible from the roadside and Hillsdown Farm to the left.

Cross the ford where the road starts to go uphill and turn right at the crossroads towards Sharpthorne and The Bluebell Railway (5). This has to be one of the quietest roads in Sussex - it is gloriously narrow and therefore often completely devoid of cars. Go downhill over a second ford, up a short sharp hill and left at the T junction. Pause at the farm gate opposite to savour the view over fine countryside.

Freewheel down the gentle incline with high hedgerows either side of this narrow road. After half a mile look for the left turn through the gate which is signposted Broadhurst Manor (6). Follow the metalled road, which is also a bridleway, and you will see the splendour of the manor-house to the left. Turn right then first left to continue along the bridleway which is now a wide track and is marked as the Sussex Border Path. The surface is firm and although parts become boggy in very wet weather it usually remains rideable. You pass many private fishing ponds to the right and left through light woodland past the church, a school and into the attractive village of Horsted Keynes.

When you emerge into the village you will be alongside The Green Man (7), a delightful Beards of Sussex pub serving excellent beer and good food in the Bluebell Bar. Horsted Keynes is the half way point of this ride and an ideal location for refreshment, either in the pub or outside on the green. Fifty yards

from the pub is the Forge North American Indian Centre and Museum - open by arrangement!

From the pub turn right and after a few hundred yards turn right at the crossroads signposted for Sharpthorne. Look at the classic timbered Sussex houses on both sides of this junction. After half a mile downhill turn left to Horsted Keynes Station. A large sign by the roadside announces that this is the home of the Bluebell Railway. Where the road bends left, turn right to the station itself and step back in history to a time when steam was king (8).

The station has been fully restored and the platforms, ticket hall and workshops are as they were in days gone by. Steam trains run from Sheffield Park, 5 miles to the south, and will hopefully in the future also run north through Sharpthorne.

On leaving the station, turn right, pass under the bridge and right at the T junction (9) onto Hammenden Lane signposted for Highbrook and West Hoathly. Pass Brook House to the left and continue through the attractive village of Highbrook where you can stop and admire the church. There are plenty of gaps in the hedgerows through which the fine views of the Sussex countryside can be appreciated. Where you pass Grovelands

Organic Farm, the lane takes on the appearance of a tunnel with trees either side meeting at the top to form a green canopy.

The road ends at a crossroads where the Vinols Cross Inn is perched on the corner. (10). It is easy to take a short diversion here to the village of West Hoathly just a few hundred yards to the left. There are many unusual buildings, particularly The Priest House & Museum and the church, opposite The Cat pub, is worth a visit. At the Vinols Cross Inn crossroads turn right into Sharpthorne. Carry straight on through the village and as you leave it the road starts uphill and you turn left signposted for East Grinstead (11).

It is downhill until you cross the western edge of the Weir Wood reservoir. There is then a short sharp climb up Stone Hill. Stop half way up in the layby on the right, and look out over the reservoir with Ashdown Forest beyond. (12) At Saint Hill, bear right towards Standen, a National Trust property with a fine house and gardens (open April to October -Weds to Sunday).

Proceed downhill for half a mile past the Tobias School of Art on the left to the suburban outskirts of East Grinstead. Pass Dunnings Mill Squash & Health club and go up the hill to a mini-roundabout at which you branch left onto Ship Street (13). Pass Portland Drive on the right and turn right at the T junction onto West Street. You are now back in East Grinstead and the church tower looms over the town over to the right. Turn immediately left at the mini-roundabout onto London Road and pass by the shops. Just before the road goes over the bypass, turn left (one way) to return to the station.

DOWNSLINK SOUTH -
TO BRAMBER & THE SOUTH DOWNS

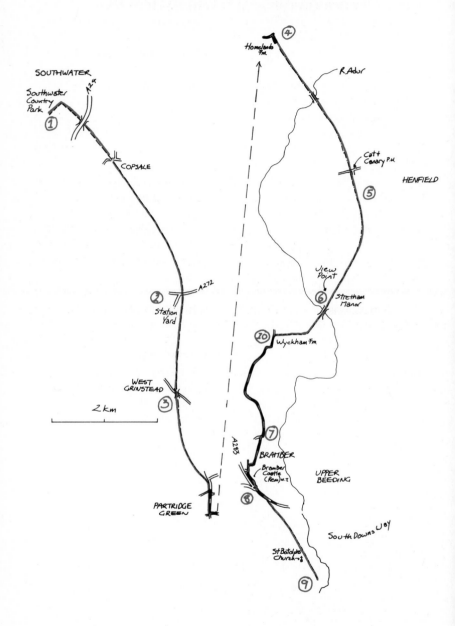

DOWNSLINK - SOUTH
TO BRAMBER & THE SOUTH DOWNS

Map	OS LR 198 Brighton and The Downs
Start	Southwater Country Park, off the A24.
Finish	Same as start.
Distance	24 miles, all off-road and flat.
Route	Follows the southern section of the Downslink along the line of a disused railway from Southwater to Bramber. The surface is generally good and although there will be sections with puddles after heavy rain, it is a firm surface. In good conditions a mountain bike is not essential.
Attractions	Henfield, River Adur Flood Meadows, Bramber Castle, Sussex Countryside.
Refreshments	The Green Man pub - Partridge Green, Cat and Canary pub, shops an Tea Rooms in Henfield. Pub and shops in Upper Beeding.

(1) Park at the Southwater Country Park car park which is clearly signposted from the A24. Turn right onto the Downslink, which runs along the edge of the car park. The route is fairly well signposted throughout but here and there you will need to look hard to spot the signs. After a short distance, pass under the A24 and then over a minor road at the one mile point.

The track stretches ahead invitingly. It is a broad path with a good surface and the riding is easy. The hedgerows contain much plant life: wild roses, daisies and hawthorn. There follows 1.5 miles of pleasant cycling interrupted only by the delights of the Sussex countryside and many rabbits on the track ahead.

After 2.5 miles pass under the A272 (2) where you ride between the long deserted platforms of West Grinstead station. This area is being developed by the council as a car park and picnic site. Carry on towards Partridge Green and cross the bridge over the B2135. At this 4 mile point a rusty collection of old farm implements and machinery lays by the side of the track (3).

Where you join the road at Partridge Green, turn right and take the second left which is about half a mile away by the 'Thank You' sign as you leave the village. It is a metalled farm track which is also a bridleway. After two hundred yards the Downslink is rejoined by turning right (4).

At 6 miles you reach a gate and cross a large open field. The remains of a WWII gun emplacement stands sentinel to the right of the track. Pause where you cross the River Adur to take in the peaceful and attractive country scene of the Adur wending its way through the flood meadows.

At 7.3 miles (5) you reach the road to the west of Henfield. The Cat & Canary pub is 20 yards to the left. Turn right then immediately left into Holland Road. At the bottom go left and look for the Downslink track signposted to the right. Rejoin the track for three delightful miles to Bramber.

If you choose to take the short diversion into the village of Henfield, go past The Cat & Canary and turn right at the T junction onto the High Street.

A conveniently placed seat provides a resting place to soak up the splendid view of the South Downs ahead, the River Adur and Chanctonbury Ring. Cross the river again at Stretham Manor (6) and leave the old railway line at the 9.5 mile point. Here the track ahead narrows and is overgrown. The Downslink continues to the right and skirts the edge of a farm field before turning left on the farm road past Wyckham Farm.

Glide down the road to the outskirts of Bramber. (7) At the T junction turn right then first left onto Kingstone Road. Cycle past the houses to the bottom and turn left at the T junction and straight on for 100 yards to a large roundabout with the A283 (8) Steyning Bypass.

To the left of the roundabout is the remains of Bramber Castle, a Norman fortress built in the late 11th Century and destroyed in the Civil War by Parliamentarians. It is now a National Trust property. Nearby Steyning, reached by turning right at the roundabout, is well worth a visit to see the timber framed buildings of the High Street and Church Street.

To complete the first half of the ride, take care in going a short distance down the A283 towards Shoreham and look for the Downslink track to the right. Rejoin the line of the old railway for the half mile ride alongside the west side of the River Adur to a seat at the base of St Botolphs, overlooking the South Downs and the river. (9)

St Botolphs Church is one of the oldest Saxon churches in Sussex. The bridge ahead over the river leads to the South Downs way, for those who feel the need for a quick blast up a steep hill! The alternative is to retrace your steps to the castle roundabout and go into Upper Beeding for refreshment. Given the level gradient of the route, the 12 miles to St Botolphs can be comfortably covered easily inside two hours.

Retrace your steps for the ride back to Southwater, looking out for the right turn off the farm road (10) to skirt the field above Wyckham Farm.

ARUNDEL & THE DOWNS

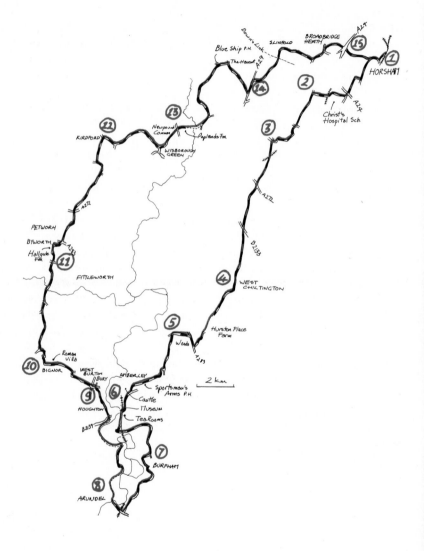

ARUNDEL & THE DOWNS

Map	OS LR 187 Dorking, Reigate and Crawley area. LR 197 Chichester and the Downs and a short straight section on LR 198 Brighton and the Downs.
Start	Horsham BR Station - Trains from Victoria via Gatwick, or Dorking (not Sundays).
Finish	Horsham BR Station.
Distance	58 miles.
Route	The route is an intricate though fairly direct crossing of Sussex. It uses the gap cut by the River Arun in the South Downs and includes only one long climb. It contains off-road riding, some on well-drained chalk downland. Most of the rest can easily be bypassed in wet weather. The route can be ridden one-way using trains from Horsham to Amberley or Arundel.
Attractions	Amberley Chalk-Pits, Arundel Town and Nature Reserve, Petchworth.
Refreshments	The Tea Rooms at Houghton Bridge are convenient in both directions. There is lots of choice in Arundel.

Horsham is an old town which prospered as a centre of iron working before the industrial revolution. Recently it has lost a lot of its charm but parts are still worth visiting. Best is The Causeway, behind the Town Hall, which runs from the town centre down towards the River Arun. Its name refers to the fact that it was once built on wooden piles above the riverside marches. The Horsham Museum at no. 9 contains lots of interesting paraphernalia of local history, including a small collection of vintage cycles.

From the Station (1) turn left down North Street (there is a café in Carfax park on your right). Turn right into Albion Way - The Causeway is found by going straight on at the bottom of North Street - then left into the Worthing Road, the B2257. Cross the river and climb out of town.

After crossing the railway bridge, turn right at the Boar's Head on the edge of town, signposted for Christs Hospital. Pass under the new Worthing Road and over the Railway to cross the DOWNSLINK RIDE. Turn left at the T junction (2) (3.5 miles) and continue over the hill into Barns Green. Keep to the right through the village and turn right just before the level crossing and left at the T junction (3) (6 miles). This lane follows a fairly direct line south through

Coneyhurst, where a left then right 'dog leg' takes it across the A272 and then to Broadford Bridge where the procedure is repeated on the B2133.

The steep chalk wall of the South Downs becomes a distant presence as West Chiltington approaches. Turn right (4) (11.5 miles) in the village at the sign for Pulborough and continue past the Queen's Head and the Windmill. Turn left at the crossroads down Nyetimber Lane. At the foot of this go straight on under the barrier onto the bridle path. Follow the path across the golf course and into the small strip of woodland. At the junction of bridleways, continue through the gate, turning left at Hurston Place Farm.

Follow the track to the metalled road and turn right. This little off-road section has crossed two side streams of the River Arun the Chilt and the Stor. On reaching the A283 turn right. At the next junction turn left, signposted Greatham and Rackham. Take the first left (5) (15.5 miles) in the woods signed for Rackham.

The South Downs are looming ahead. Take the second right, signed for the Sportsman's Arms, and follow the road through Amberley with the steep scarp on your left. The mediaeval castle in Amberley, a private residence, was built at the northern entrance to the gap cut in the South Downs by the River Arun when the river was navigable. Today it still towers impressively above the marshes. Turn right at the T junction with the B2139 and follow it to Amberley Station at Houghton Bridge. Here there are tea-rooms and an excellent open-air industrial museum at the chalk-pits. The museum includes a newly-opened working workshop building horse-drawn carts which has been transported here - like yourself - from Horsham.

If you are feeling tired, cross the bridge to rejoin the route north. If you do this, you will cut off the most strenuous section of the route but also the most rewarding, so an alternative would be to carry on and entrain at Arundel Station. Immediately after the railway bridge, turn left (6) (20 miles) towards North Stoke. Turn left at the telephone box, cross the railway and climb the spur of the Downs as far as the barn. Follow the track which curves away to the right as you pass the sign prohibiting motor-traffic.

At Peppering High Barn Farm go straight on onto the metalled road. Turn left at Peppering Farm and continue into Burpham and turn right (7) (24 miles) after the George and Dragon and right

again at the T junction to follow the road through Warningcamp to the T junction with the A27. Turn right and cross the flats to Arundel.

Arundel has many attractions. Squeezed between the South Downs and River, its High Street is the steepest in England. The town is further constricted by the Castle. This was built by the Normans but was almost destroyed during the Civil War and is mostly 19th century reconstruction. It is open to the public (0903 883136). The town has two museums: one on local history and the other an eclectic collection of toys and militaria. The Arundel Wildfowl Trust (0903 883355) have an extensive reserve on the river flats close to the town. The town has a good range of eating places.

The route out of town (8) (26.5 miles) is just above the roundabout at the end of the bridge leading back to the railway station. Turn north up the road signposted to the Castle and Wildlife Trust. Go past the Castle entrance, Swanbourne Lake and into the no-through-road beyond the Black Rabbit. Turn left at the T junction for South Stoke. Just before South Stoke Farm turn left on to a bridleway and follow it, keeping left behind the farm buildings. Turn right through the gate and follow the bridleway along the edge of the field - watch out for rabbit holes. Through the gate and into the woods where the hazards are tree roots. This is mostly rideable but requires care, especially when the ground is wet. The woods are so delightful that to walk and linger is a pleasure.

Through the metal gate, the path rejoins the solid road-way which leads to Houghton and the B2139. This is where short cutters will join the route home and it is only a short distance across the river if you want to (re)visit the Houghton Bridge tea-rooms. To carry on, turn right (9) (31 miles) and left towards Bury. In Bury, turn left at the crossroads. Follow the signs for West Burton, crossing the A29 at a staggered, right left crossroads. In West Burton turn left for Bignor.

One of the largest Roman Villas known to have been built in Britain was discovered in 1811 on the hillside on the right as Bignor is approached. The remains, which include fragments of a huge mosaic, are open for inspection (079878 259).

Turn right (10) (34.5 miles) in the village following signs for Sutton. In Sutton turn right at the White Horse Inn. At the crossroads, go straight on, signed for Petworth and cross the River Rother, a Western tributary of the Arun.

At the staggered crossroads (11) (38.5 miles) go on towards Byworth unless you want to visit Petworth House, Park or town in which case you should go left then first right. Petworth is a small town of narrow streets and old buildings centred on an old market square. It is well worth visiting. The adjacent House and Park are on a splendid scale. The grounds were landscaped by Capability Brown and the House, which mostly dates from the 17th Century, is large and ostentatious and contains many art treasures, notably by Turner who was a frequent visitor.

In Byworth turn right by the buildings of Hallgate Farm, identified by their grey doors and slit windows, onto a track through the farmyard. Keep left into the sunken lane and emerge on the A283 at the Welldigger. Cross the A283 and then the A272, following the lane to Kirdford. After the Halfmoon keep right (12) (43.5 miles) and ride on to Wisborough Green. Go straight on at the crossroads near the Cricketers in Wisborough Green following the signs for Newpound.

At the cross roads with the B2133 (13) (47 miles) in Newpound go straight on, onto a bridleway. At the private entrance to Raplands Farm, take the unsurfaced section to the gate and then veer right towards the farm buildings across the valley. Remember to close all the gates as you cross, first a restored section of the Wey - Arun Canal and then the Arun itself. The canal once connected the Thames to the Channel. Follow the bridleway through the farm yard to the metalled road. Turn left and continue to the T junction by the 'Blue Ship'. Turn right and at the Old Post Office in The Haven turn right again to reach the A29 - Stane Street - running Roman straight across the Weald.

Turn left and first right (14) (52.5 miles). Just before Slinfold is a second crossing of the DOWNS LINK. In Slinfold turn right for Broadbridge Heath. Turn left onto the A264. At the roundabout go straight across into Broadbridge Heath Village. The next roundabout (15) (56 miles) has a cycle path through the centre into the Guildford Road. If you want to make a walking shortcut, turn left into the park. Otherwise, follow the signs for the town centre and then the station (1) (58 miles).

DOWNSLINK NORTH -
THROUGH SUSSEX & SURREY TO
ST. MARTHA'S HILL

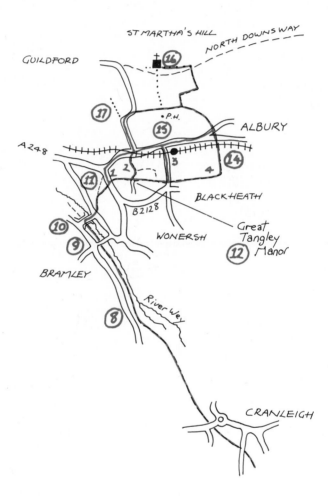

DOWNSLINK NORTH -
THROUGH SUSSEX & SURREY TO
ST. MARTHA'S HILL

Vachery Pond

Baynards Station
10 miles

Thurlow Arms P.H.

⑦

⑥

Sussex Border Path

RUDGWICK

A281

River Arun

⑤

Two-Tiered Bridge

SLINFOLD

A264

A24

A29

④ ③

②

Christs Hospital

P.H.

①

SOUTHWATER

A24

DOWNSLINK - NORTH
THROUGH SUSSEX & SURREY
TO ST. MARTHA'S HILL

Map	LR 187 start, LR 186 end.
Start	At Christs Hospital or Horsham station if arriving by train. Car parking at Southwater Country Park, reached from the A24 and clearly signposted. It is possible to start this ride at Guildford, Chilworth or at Southwater.
Finish	Half way is 21.5 miles at Chilworth at the base of St Martha's Hill. You could return by train from here or complete the round trip.
Distance	46m from Southwater to the top of St Martha's Hill and back, all off-road. Allow a full day for the ride.
Route	A level route following the course of a disused railway with a couple of inclines as you approach the North Downs and Chilworth. The climb up St Martha's Hill is demanding but short, taking 20 minutes from Chilworth.
Sights	Christs Hospital, Rudgwick Village, Baynards Station, North Downs, St. Martha's Hill.
Refreshment	Thurlow Arms at Baynards Station - there is also a picnic site opposite the pub. Percy Arms at Chilworth (half way). Bax Castle, one mile before the finish at Southwater.

The Downslink is a bridleway linking the North Downs Way with the South Downs Way. It follows disused branch railway lines for most of the way. It is a level, clearly signposted bridleway and is maintained by the Local Authorities. This section of the link offers a full day ride along magnificent stretches of uninterrupted cycling through the charming countryside of Surrey and Sussex. There is the option of a demanding but short climb up St Martha's Hill. It is possible to treat this route as an all day round trip, starting from north or south, or just to complete one section.

Christs Hospital is the nearest railway station, 3 km from Horsham. Pick up the Downslink path 300 yards south of the station. If arriving by car, park at the Southwater Country Park (1) which was opened in 1985 on the site of a famous brickworks and has a small lake providing a popular venue for the sailing of radio controlled yachts. The Downslink is easily located alongside the car park.

Ride north long the track towards Christs Hospital, passing under the first of many bridges. There are as many gates on this short stretch as there are on the rest of the 20 miles to Chilworth. The path skirts the playing fields of Christs Hospital, the famous Bluecoat school. The governors moved to this site at the turn of the century in order to escape the pollution in London. It is apt that the Downslink allows other city dwellers to do just that, albeit only for the day.

The path joins the road 20 yards from the railway bridge (2) to the left, under which the main line heads south to the coast and north to London. Turn left and go over the bridge to the T junction at which you turn right. A short way along is a sharp left hand bend at which you turn right off the road at Baystone House. Look for the Downslink signpost on the side of the road. Fifty yards up the tarmac road turn left onto the Downslink.

At every junction, whether with track, footpath or road, the route is waymarked on tall sign posts or short ground posts. The logo is a graphic representation of a two tiered bridge.

There follows a pleasant ride along a single track towards Slinfold through the Low Weald (3). Woodpeckers are sometimes seen in this area and there is an abundance of attractive wild flowers including cowslips, splendid primroses in Spring, and honeysuckle which attracts butterflies. The attractive village of Slinfold is worth a detour and is less than one mile from the Link.

Turn right off the Link at the junction with Hayes Lane (4), at which there is a gate and a house with an old advertisement still visible on the wall. Proceed up Hayes Lane then turn left along The Street to reach the village centre with the customary pub, church and old cottages. Retrace the route or turn left again down Spring Lane to rejoin the Link at the caravan park on the site of the old station.

You then reach the A29 (5) (a Roman Road from Chichester to London) and go straight on to enjoy a delightful few miles to the two tiered bridge over the River Arun which gives the Downslink its distinctive logo. The higher bridge was built because the railway inspector wanted to overcome the steep gradient to the nearby station at Rudgwick. Cross the A281 and at the next bridge you can turn right for a 1.5 mile detour to Rudgwick Village, which has a church tower dating from the mid 12th century.

You then reach a bricked up tunnel (6) and the path veers left up a short sharp incline to join the Sussex Border Path. Turn left for a short distance where the path levels off then look for a right turn to a nice downhill stretch through light woodland to the road. Turn right on the road over the bridge and then double back under the bridge to rejoin the track bed.

In a short distance you will reach Baynards Station (7) with the Thurlow arms opposite. You will have covered 10 miles and be roughly half way to Chilworth.

The Thurlow Arms has good food and drink with a garden and there is a picnic area opposite for those who prefer self catering. Baynards Station is privately owned, lived in, intact and remarkably well-preserved. The platform buildings are in better shape than they were when the last train ran through here in the summer of 1965. Remember that it is someone's home so gawp from the Downslink rather than from the top of the fence. The entrance to Baynards Estate is here - it is also private. You can look at the old station and imagine the fine and mighty coming down from town for a weekend at Baynards House.

There follows a good stretch that goes past Vachery pond, round the west of Cranleigh, and over the road to a long uninterrupted ride of 5 miles to Bramley and Wonersh. The Link passes over attractive open countryside with common pastures used for grazing horses.

The Wey and Arun canal, (8) built in the early part of the

1800s, runs parallel to the Link and was effectively closed by the railway in the late 1860s. Towards the end of this stretch you can see to the left an architectural salvage yard full of the features of yesteryear, from flagstones to Victorian chimney pots.

At Bramley (9) you cross a road at the site of the old Wonersh & Bramley Station. The station name plate remains as does the platform and you can choose whether to cycle along the platform or on the track bed for fifty yards or so.

At the 19 mile point you turn right at a bridge (10) (a footpath goes straight on) to join the road for 50 yards to the T junction and go straight on at a property called Southlands. The North Downs are before you. Continue up a short incline to a view point at the west of Chinthurst Hill affording magnificent views of the surrounding countryside. The metropolis of Guildford is clearly visible to the north-west, the North Downs are to the front with Martha's Hill ahead. Follow the blue arrow on the post and take the track down to the right. This portion of the route can be boggy in wet weather.

At the road junction (B2128) (11) you will see the turning for the A248 to Dorking and Albury to the left and the Link

continuing across the road. Keep a sharp eye for the Downslink symbol on the sign posts from now on, as the clarity of the disused railway has been left behind and there are a number of options from here. The road route to Chilworth (option 1 on the map) is favourite if your legs are weary and you need lunch. Take the turning for Dorking and Albury and one mile along the road on the left is The Percy Arms, opposite the railway station.

There are three other choices to get to Chilworth from the junction of the B2128 and A248. Instead of following the road to Chilworth go straight on to continue on the Downslink bridleway for 400 metres to Great Tangley Manor Farm.

There is a crossroads here (12) and a left turn (option two on the map) will take you past Brooks Woods to the Chilworth-Albury road. Turn right and The Percy Arms is a few hundred metres on the left. If you go straight on at Tangley Manor Farm you will be following the Downslink proper (option 3) which goes slightly uphill through the Blackheath woods.

Where the bridleway meets the road, (13) a signpost points the way to Blackheath village to the right. Turn left onto the road and revel in a long downhill glide which brings you out directly opposite the pub. There is an interesting monastery to the left. This is the best route to Chilworth as it offers the nice climb through Blackheath and the short road stretch downhill is infinitely more satisfying than the main road option.

True aficionados of the Downslink will continue straight on at the road to Blackheath (14) (option 4 on the map) for the pleasant downhill section through the woods along the bridleway to Lockner Lodge. Cross over the railway to the A248 where a left takes you to the pub and straight on past Lockner Farm goes to St Martha's Hill.

It is about three hours or so to here, (15) so relax a while at the Percy Arms. The pleasant gardens at the base of the North Downs is a good spot from which to contemplate whether to go the top of St Martha's or not.

There is a certain satisfaction in getting to the top, but it is not an easy ride, boggy in the wet and difficult sand in the dry. It is only twenty minutes from the pub. If you decide to go for it, turn left out of the pub and left after 500m up the bridleway at Lockner Farm. The climb is over 1 km and a touch stiff, as much to do with the surface as the gradient. The

track joins the North Downs Way slightly to the east of the Hill and go left before this to reach the actual top.

On the summit is St Martha's Church (16), originally Norman but rebuilt in the 19th century. You will have to walk the last 100m to the top as it is a footpath.

There is a preferred route back to the disused railway to avoid climbing back up to Blackheath on the road or Downslink proper. Follow the bridleway back down from St Martha's and turn right (west) instead of left along the track you followed up past Lockner Farm.

After 500m the bridleway (17) joins a minor road where a right turn goes to Guildford and a left goes downhill to Chilworth. At the junction with the A248 turn right and after 100m turn left onto the bridleway at Tangley Mere (option 2 on the way up). After nearly 200m turn right along the top of Brooks Wood up the track (boggy in the wet) to Great Tangley Manor Farm. At the farm is a crossroads at which you turn right. Cross the B2128 and climb round the base of Chinthurst Hill to the road T junction. Go straight on down the road for 50m and turn left at the bridge to rejoin the Downslink track.

LEITH HILL & THE WEALD

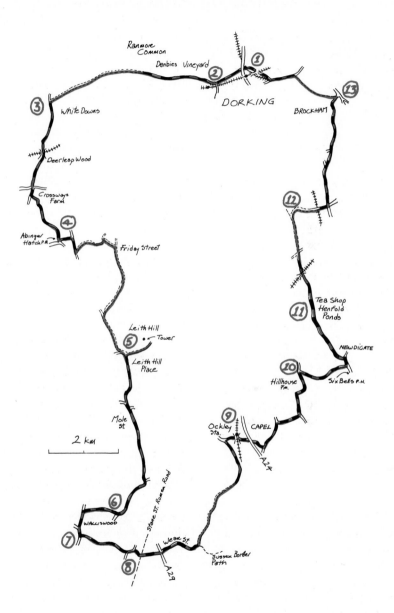

LEITH HILL & THE SURREY WEALD

Map	OS LR 187 Dorking, Reigate and Crawley Area.
Start	Dorking BR Station. Trains approximately 50 minutes from Victoria and Waterloo carry cycles, except with the rush hour flow. The A24 from Leatherhead has a cycle lane. There is car parking at the station. Train information - Victoria 071 928 5100 or Brighton 0273 206755. An adjacent but separate station, Dorking Deepdene, has connections to Gatwick, Redhill, Guildford and Reading as above.
Finish	Dorking BR Station.
Distance	30.5 miles.
Route	The route runs west from Dorking, climbs to Ranmore Common, then down and up to Leith Hill on the southernmost ridge of the North Downs. It then plunges into the wet oak woods of the Surrey Weald and returns to Dorking by a much more level Mole Valley. It is all on road apart from a short, well-drained bridleway shortcut near the end. There is a good deal of steep climbing in the first 10 miles.
Attractions	Ranmore Common, Leith Hill, the oak wood villages and hammer pond of the Weald.
Refreshments	Dorking has several pubs and cafés. There are teas at Leith Hill and Henfold Ponds and many village pubs on route, notably the Six Bells in Newdigate.

As late as the 1890's, in 'The Reigate Puzzle', Conan Doyle had Dr. Watson prescribe a week in the Surrey Hills 'the depths of the country' for a sickly Sherlock Holmes. A resident of Norwood, between Crystal Palace and Croydon, and a keen cyclist, Doyle was familiar with the lanes this route follows.

Leave Dorking Station (1) and turn right onto the A24. Turn left immediately onto the Ashcombe Road which bypasses the town and is signed for Guildford. At the roundabout (2) (0.5 miles) fork right and then turn right again at the T junction onto Ranmore Road.

If you want to start this ride by visiting Dorking town you can substitute the Start of the BOX HILL route which brings you to the roundabout from the other side to fork left into Ashcombe Road and then right into Ranmore. This is a long drag up onto the North Downs but you are rewarded with ever-expanding views over Dorking and the flatter ride across the wooded heights of Ranmore Common which follows.

Just past Ranmore Lodge a trackway forks off to the right. If you follow this, you will reach White Downs Road, where you should turn left. If you want to stay on the road, carry on 500m to the crossroads (3) (3.5 miles)

and turn left into White Downs Road which is signed for Abinger. Either way takes you uphill to the wooded crest of the Downs. The road runs through a short cutting at the top and a long steep descent follows to cross the Guildford Road into Raikes Lane by Crossways Farm. The little river is the Tilling Bourne running west to join the Wey at Guildford. Just across it turn left at the signpost for Abinger Common.

The mile climb that follows is neither as long or as steep as the previous descent and you have the benefit of shade. Turn left at the top (4) (6.5 miles) just past the Abinger Hatch Pub, into a rather indistinct road that looks like a private drive. At the T junction at the bottom, turn right and then left at the signpost for Friday Street, an exquisite wooded hamlet with pub on the shores of a small lake.

Beyond, go straight on as a road merges from the left, following the sign for Leith Hill. Turn left at the T junction signed for Ockley and Coldharbour. Half a mile further on a path leads through the woods on your left (5) (10 miles). Although there is a shorter path from the road to the summit of Leith Hill on the other side, it is much steeper.

Leith Hill is the highest point in South East England at 294m and if you pay the small admission charge, you can climb the tower on the top to reach 1,000 feet above sea-level. The detour is well worth, it particularly on a fine day when you can see over an area of 200 square miles. It is possible to see the water of the Channel through the South Downs at the Shoreham Gap. Teas are served at the bottom of the tower in summer.

On returning to the road, continue down over the crossroads past Leith Hill Place, where the composer Ralph Vaughan Williams once lived. At the T junction turn left onto the B2136 for Ockley. Turn right with care at the junction on the next bend into Mole Street, which takes you down into the Surrey Weald.

The Weald lies between the North and South Downs in the counties of Surrey, Sussex and Kent and is a mysterious place. It is made of soft clay and harder sandstone. The clay has worn into flat wet valleys while the sandstone ridges are in places almost as high as the Downs to north and south. The streams you are crossing now run south into the River Arun and Chichester Harbour. Oakwood Church is hidden in woods to the left and makes a quiet stopping place.

Near the turn-off for the Church (6) (13.5 miles) is Black

and White Cottage, the Hannah Pescher Gallery which is open at weekends in summer. At the Scarlett Arms pub, turn left into Walliswood. Turn left at the signpost (7) (14.5 miles) for Oakwoodhill and in the village go straight on past the Punchbowl Inn. Fork right at the next junction in the village.

Where this road bends to the left (8) (16 miles) it crosses the Roman Road from London to Chichester which the Saxons called Stane Street - the track on the right shows its line. The Romans built two other roads across the Weald, one to Brighton and one to Lewes. They did not settle here.

At the A29, the present Chichester road, cross over into Weare Street, which climbs gradually along a shallow wooded valley. Athough it lacks the grandeur of some of the downland lanes to the north it is one of Surrey's finest. This is the southern limit of the ride. The Sussex border is a few hundred yards on the right.

Turn right at the T junction (9) (19 miles) and continue past Ockley Railway Station which has hourly trains for Dorking and London, and on to cross the A24. Ockley, Okewood, Okehill...these Saxon place names identify the area's dominant plant, the oak tree, 'the weed of the weald'.

At the T junction with the old Worthing road, turn left to follow it north through the village of Capel. Turn right by the garage signed for Charlwood and Newdigate. Follow this road as it zig-zags north east to a T junction (10) (21.5 miles) on the edge of the village of Beare Green, and turn right following the sign for Newdigate. Enter Newdigate down Trig Street. Greens Farm, which is seen to the right, has stood since the 13th Century.

This area was known a hundred years ago as the loneliest place in Surrey. The heavy clay soil of the area meant the green lanes that connected it to the outside world were often impassable even in summer. There are many old farms and cottages, built with frames of local oak. Even the Church has a timber tower.

Turn left at the T junction in Newdigate and left again up Henfold Lane, signposted for Dorking and Holmwood. In the wet valleys of the Weald the rivers which flow north and south interlock. We can now follow the Mole back to Dorking, so the last quarter of the ride is mostly downhill. It passes a series of lakes, first Henfold Ponds (11) (24 miles) where there is a Tea Shop after a steep

descent (it is easy to overshoot) then Fourwents Pond.

These are 'hammer ponds', relics of the iron industry which flourished here in the sixteenth and seventeenth centuries. Local iron ore was smelted using wood-burning furnaces and the ponds were constructed to create a head of water to power bellows and hammers. This iron was used mostly for armaments and the industry caused rapid deforestation which only halted when coal mining and canals switched the centre of iron working to the Black Country of the West Midlands.

After Fourwents Ponds follow the signs for Leigh and Brockham, turning right then right again at a T junction (12) (25.5 miles). Cross the railway and turn left to run downhill to Brockham. Excellent tea and cake at the village hall here on Sunday afternoons (May to September). If you do not want to go into the village, turn left (13) (28 miles) just before the bridge onto a well-drained bridlepath across a golf course. Turn left on the main Reigate Road and right onto Pixham Lane. Turn left at the roundabout on the London Road to return to the Station (1) (30.5 miles).

MOLE VALLEY & BOX HILL -
THE ROMANTICS RETREAT

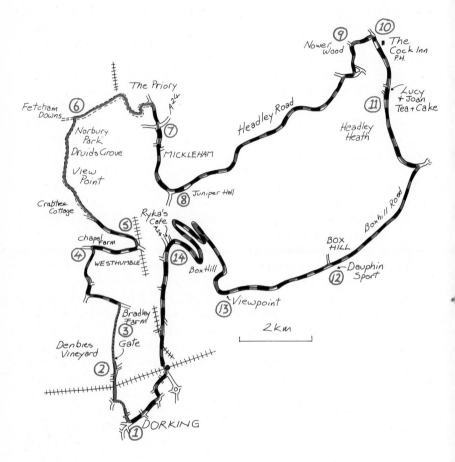

MOLE VALLEY & BOX HILL - THE ROMANTIC'S RETREAT

Map	OS LR 187 Dorking, Reigate and Crawley Area.
Start	Dorking BR Station. Trains from Victoria and Waterloo carry cycles except with the rush hour flow. The A24 from Leatherhead has a cycle lane. Car parking at the station. Train information - Victoria 071 928 5100 or Brighton 0273 206755.
Finish	Dorking BR Station.
Distance	16 miles.
Route	The route runs north from Dorking on high ground west of the River Mole, crosses the river and loops round to approach Box Hill from the east before dropping back to the valley to return to Dorking. There is a little walking in the first two miles and the off-road riding is all on good tracks. There are several hills but only one is steep.
Attractions	Denbies Vineyard, Norbury Park, Mickleham Village, Box Hill.
Refreshments	Dorking has several pubs and cafés. Teas at Chapel Farm, Headley Village and Box Hill. The Running Horses in Mickleham serves food. La Collina (073 784 2338) a licensed Italian restaurant on top of Box Hill. Meals at Burford Bridge at Ryka's café or the Burford Bridge Hotel.

This short route is a fine introduction to the charm of the North Downs. The popularity of the area as a retreat for romantics and a playground for the vigorous is undiminished in the hundred and ninety years since Jane Austen had Emma say... 'We are going to Boxhill tomorrow: you will join us. It is not Swisserland, but it will be something for a young man so much in want of a change.'

From Dorking Station (1) ride down Station Approach to the A24 London Road and turn left. Pass under the railway bridge and turn right after the Esso Garage. This quiet lane, London Road, was the radial route to Dorking before the motor age. Its scale gives you an idea of the town's remoteness before the coming of the railway.

As the London Road emerges into the High Street, turn right. The centre of the town is pleasantly unimproved but the one-way system means it is best explored on foot. West Street is particularly charming with rows of wonky old buildings. If it's not a Sunday, a visit to the Belgian Patisserie on the High Street is recommended. There is a little museum in West Street open on Wednesday, Thursday and Saturday afternoons. The glimpses of high hills around the town give the place an alpine feeling.

At the Junction of High Street and West Street find the narrow lane North Street and go down it, passing the old pump house and crossing the bridge. The lane shrinks to a footpath. At the T junction by the electricity sub-station turn left. Where the path emerges onto Chalkpit Lane, turn right up the hill. As Chalkpit Lane bears right, continue up Yew Tree Road and then fork onto the rising footpath. This steep shaded path will bring you to the crest of the hill and the unexpected sight of a 250 acre vineyard. From here you can also survey, on the right, our ultimate objective, Box Hill.

Lift your bike over the metal gate (2) (1.2 miles) and walk down among the newly planted vines. The Denbies Wine Estate has spread eastward from its original base along the south-facing slope of the North Downs, where the poor flint and chalk soil, and the sheltered aspect, is ideal for viticulture. It is now Britain's largest vineyard. Look out for the labels on the plants which give the names of the grape varieties. The big new Winery building lying ahead near the old Bradley's Farm (3) is open for tasting and sales 10:30-18:00 and 12:00 - 17:30 Sundays. You may want to come back with a trailer. If you have been down to the winery, retrace your route to the crossing of footpath and bridleway just above the old farm buildings and take the bridleway up the hill towards the woods. Riding is now permitted so you can, if you wish, try. As the path enters the wood it gets steeper and when it reaches the North Downs Way turn right.

At the fork in the track, bear left and follow the gentle descent to Chapel Farm. (4) (2.5 miles) Turn right. On your right stands a flint gable wall, all that remains of a 12th Century chapel which fell into disuse at the end of the middle ages. Steps from the lane give access to the overgrown site where you can examine the remaining foundations or sit in the shade of the yews. Across the road the farm is open March 1st - October 31st, 10:00 -17:00. (tel. 0306 882 865) It is popular with children and has a tea shop.

Run down through West Humble Village. Just before the bridge make a sharp left turn into Crabtree Lane to the right of the gateway marked 'Leladine' (5). Fanny Burney built a house near here, with the profits from her third novel 'Camilla', published in 1796. In those days, the novel was not a respectable form; new, decadent and popular. Think of computer games.

Our next destination, Norbury Park House is visible through the trees up to your right. Up Crabtree Lane then turn right, signposted Norbury Park Estate,

Surrey County Council. The wooded grounds contain a network of bridleways and a collection of sculpture (tel Clare Holloway 081 541 9179). As the road climbs towards the house it offers fine views down to the Mole Gap. The sign to the right for Druids Grove Viewpoint leads to an avenue of ancient Yew trees.

The road passes a saw mill, and runs behind the imposing house, (6) (5 miles) which remains a private residence, before dropping back down to the valley. The downhill has unmarked speed-bumps and a sharp lefthand bend so take care. The London bound railway passes under this road in a tunnel. A condition of its construction in 1848 was that it should remain hidden from the house.

At the T junction by the priory turn right and cross the river and the A24 to enter Mickleham village (7) on the Old London Road. Pass through the village, and at Juniper Hall (8) (7 miles), owned by the National Trust and run as a Natural History Study Centre, turn left up Headley Road. Some of the most distinguished emigrés from the French revolution stayed at Juniper Hall in the 1790's, including Talleyrand and General D'Arblay, who married

Fanny Burney at Mickleham Church.

Headley Road is known locally as little Switzerland, winding up the steep vale between White Hill and Box Hill for two of Surrey's most pleasant miles. At the T junction turn right then left into Tumber Street. This rural lane bears right into Slough Lane (9) (9.5 miles). Turn left here if you wish to detour to rest in Nower Wood, otherwise at the T junction you can turn right on the road or use the short bridleway which brings you up past the Cock Inn (10).

Beside the village stores on your left, Lucy and Joan serve tea and homemade cakes at weekends throughout the year and all week in summer. Look for the 'Village Teas' sign. Go straight on through the village onto Headley Heath. If the tea shop was closed, a caravan stall (11) (10 miles) on the right, opposite the cricket ground, is open all year.

Turn sharp right into Box Hill Road which takes you out along the top of the ridge through the resort of Box Hill with a chalet park on the right, and several big pubs. The popularity of the area with cyclists supports Dauphin Sport (12) (12 miles) - open 09:00 till 18:00, Monday-Saturday - a shop which sells lightweight bikes, components and flashy

clothing to the velo-sportifs who come to train on Box Hill's hairpins. If you are feeling inspired and ambitious, it has a list of the Surrey Divisions Racing clubs posted outside. The road bends at Donkey Green, where children could buy rides in earlier times. The Hill was given to the National Trust in 1914 and there is a shop and information centre as well as a café (11:00 -16:00 all year round) near the pre-historic fort. From the viewpoint (13) (13 miles) below the road you can see 24 miles across the Weald. You can also see Dorking Station barely a mile away but 500ft below.

Botanists once thought that the groves of box trees with their smooth bark, corkscrew stems and shaggy crowns of pungent evergreen leaves, were planted in Roman times for their valuable timber. Recent finds of box charcoal in Neolithic camps in the South Downs suggest that it is a native species whose dislike of our wet seasonal climate restricts it to a few locations. These south-facing slopes are not only a well drained sun-trap but their steepness has always protected the trees from over-exploitation.

On the descent, the sleeping-policemen are clearly marked, visible even through wind-induced tears. The groves of box trees are typical of the limestone gorges of France, so are the smooth hairpins. We rejoin the Old London Road and turn right to pass the Burford Bridge Hotel (14) (15 miles) where Keats wrote Endymion. The grandeur of the setting draws romantics like a magnet.

The Hotel serves teas until 17:30, then the restaurant is open until 22:30. Opposite the Hotel is Ryka's Café ('Burgers, we're famous for them') open from 08:00 to 24:00.

On reaching the A24, turn left and follow the cycle track back to Dorking (1) (16 miles). On a path to the left you can break your journey again, by walking down to the stepping stones on the North Downs Way to sit by the water and take another perspective on Box Hill.

THE THAMES FROM PUTNEY
TO HAMPTON COURT

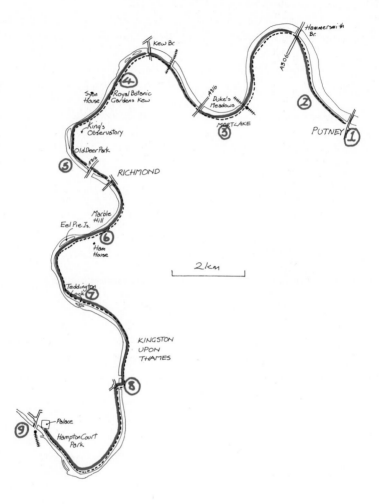

THE THAMES FROM PUTNEY TO HAMPTON COURT

Map	OS LR 176 West London area.
Start	Putney Bridge. Get there from central London via the King's Road.
Finish	Hampton Court. Trains to Waterloo from Hampton Court. A boat service runs from Westminster to Hampton Court with stops at Putney, Kew and Richmond. Bikes are carried free of charge. Information 071 930 2062 or 081 892 0741.
Distance	16 miles. The surface of the path varies but bumpy sections are neither prolonged nor severe. It can be easily ridden on a road-bike shod with 32mm (1 inch) touring tyres. After wet weather it holds shallow puddles but is generally well-drained, firm and even.
Route	The towpath is primarily a walking route, but the National Rivers Authority welcomes careful cycling along this section. The pedestrian flows on summer weekends can be heavy near vehicle access points, making cycling neither pleasant nor practical. On an overcast winter weekday you can go for miles without meeting a soul.
Attractions	Kew Gardens, Syon House, Richmond, Richmond Park, Bushy Park, Ham House, Petersham, Hampton Court Palace.
Refreshments	Tea shop in Richmond Park, riverside pubs at Richmond and Kingston. Ham House.

The Thames as a barrier to land travel and a corridor for shipping justifies London. The city grew up around the only place where gravel beds on both banks provide good footings for bridges, quays and buildings and where the river's tidal waters can accommodate ocean going craft. Trading vessels were landing before the Roman conquest and sea-going traffic continued until less than thirty years ago. From Saxon times, barges plied up-river to Oxford and inland trade peaked as canals linking the Thames to Bristol, Birmingham and the South Coast opened in the late 18th century.

Start the path from the Surrey (south) end of Putney Bridge outside the Star and Garter pub. (1) Pass the slipways where if you are lucky you will see crews of oarsmen and women silently perfecting their technique in the tideway. A footbridge crosses Beverley Brook (2 miles) which rises in Sutton and flows between Wimbledon Common and Richmond Park. The beavers were hunted out a long time ago.

At Mortlake (3) (3.5 miles) the Young's Stag Brewery backs onto the river and the iron rails in the cobbles show where trucks brought the beer barrels to the quay for loading. Pass the sewage plant and the Public Record Office. At Kew Bridge there is a river boat station where

you can check the times of boats for a return journey. At Kew you pass the Royal Botanic Gardens on your left, a nice place to linger in fine weather. Low flying cormorants and the muddy, water-worn beaches between the tide-lines give the river a maritime atmosphere, even though the sea is 35 miles away.

Opposite Kew (4) (6 miles) on the Middlesex (north) bank you can see the deep lock which gives entry to Great Western Docks and the Grand Union Mainline with connections to Birmingham, Northampton, the Wash, the Trent and the Humber. The River Brent joins the Thames here. Brentford, on the Bath Road, was the site in 1642 of one of the first battles of the Civil War. The King's men were victorious and set out to march on the City only to meet more successful resistance on Turnham Green later in the day, which saved London for Parliament. In the days when land travel was slow and hazardous, the Thames was a safe and rapid corridor and all along the banks above London are palaces and grand houses.

Beyond Kew, Syon House comes into view across the river. Syon Park was the site of a monastery before it was annexed by the crown after the split with Rome. Maybe the monks, or wife five Katherine Howard, imprisoned here before her execution, cursed Henry VIII, because when his body rested here on the way up from Westminster to Windsor, the coffin burst open in the night and dogs were discovered enjoying the remains. The House and Park were given to Earls of Northumberland by Elizabeth I. Inigo Jones, Robert Adam and Capability Brown have all worked on them. The Park contains the National Garden Centre which is open all year round and the House is open in summer (not Mondays and Tuesdays).

Syon Park can be reached by diverting over Kew Bridge and left down the A315, the old road for the west and south west (Information 081 560 0881). Isleworth Ait lies opposite Old Deer Park. ('Ait' or 'eyot' is a local word for a small island.) The two channels of the Crane enter here and beyond, the Thames in its last tidal miles is noticeably smaller. The white building seen through the trees on your left is the King's Observatory built in 1768 and in use by the Meteorological Office until 1981. Richmond Lock (5) (8 miles), technically a half-lock, which also includes a footbridge to the Middlesex bank, was built in 1890 after dredging downstream let the tide ebb faster leaving Richmond with nothing but mud at low tide. In summer the barrier is lowered twice a day to keep the last three miles of tideway full.

Richmond's grand promenade may mean a dismount. The 1777 bridge is one of the most elegant on the river. The riverfront around it was redeveloped in the 1980's, with new building styled to match the old. If you want to detour into the wide open spaces of Richmond Park go up Water Lane and turn right up Hill Street and keep left as it turns into Richmond Hill to the Richmond Gate.

Beyond the bridge, Richmond Hill dominates the scene as formal gardens give way to pastoral Petersham Meadows (6) (10 miles). Marble Hill Park on the Middlesex bank can be reached by the novelty of a ferry. This motor launch is operated by Mr Stan Rust on demand from 10:00 till 18:00 (18:30 at weekends): the ride costs 30p.

Ham House stands on the Surrey side. It is almost unaltered since the 17th century and its furnishings and formal gardens have been restored. It is open to the public and has a garden tea-house. Petersham Church holds the grave of Captain George Vancouver, who sailed with Cook to the Pacific then made his home here inland where the tide just reaches.

Upstream of Richmond, the path becomes more rural in character, overgrown with hedges, and passes Eel Pie Island, now private, which 30 years ago boasted a famous music club. Emerging at Teddington we reach the lock and weir (7) (12 miles) which mark the limit of the tidal river. Beyond is the inland Thames of Jerome K. Jerome and Kenneth Graham.

Kingston Upon Thames (8) (14.5 miles) is gutted by a one-way systems but when approached along the river its traffic free centre can still be recognised as a Surrey town at the mouth of the Hogsmill River. Halfords in the Market Square is open seven days a week if you need to replenish your puncture kit.

Cross Kingston Bridge and follow the sloping driveway which skirts Hampton Court Park in a sweeping bend. Arriving at Hampton Court Palace (9) (16 miles) on the river, as visitors were always meant to do, its scale is undiminished by subsequent development. Among riverside country retreats, only Windsor Castle is more opulent. The house and grounds have many attractions including the famous privet-hedge maze, Real Tennis courts and the kitchens, halls and apartments of the Palace (information 081 781 9500). If you want more pastoral pleasures, Bushy Park across the Green is expansive and quite under-used.

WINDSOR, THE GREAT PARK
& VIRGINIA WATER

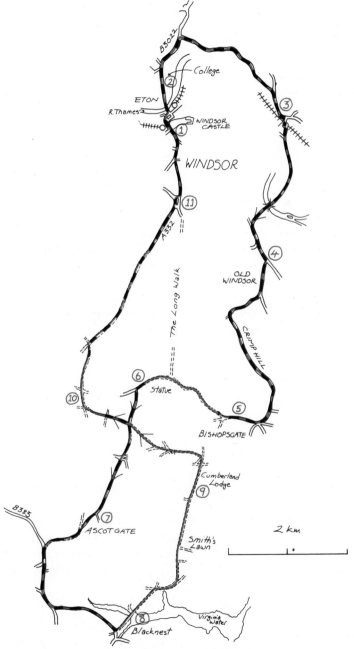

WINDSOR, THE GREAT PARK
& VIRGINIA WATER

Map	OS LR 175 Reading and Windsor, has the whole route. LR 176 West London covers almost all the route.
Start	Windsor Guildhall in Windsor Town Centre. Windsor has two railway stations nearby with services from Paddington, Victoria or Waterloo. Car parking is easiest at Blacknest Gate allowing you to start the route from there. Cycle from London via Teddington, Sunbury and Staines.
Finish	Windsor Guildhall.
Distance	17 miles all on tarmac - only one significant hill.
Route	After following the Thames downstream, this ride climbs into Windsor Great Park. It crosses the park east to west then loops round to cross it south to north returning to Windsor. A bicycling monarch - as in Sweden or the Netherlands - may be tabloid shorthand for much reduced circumstances, but if it does come to that, the House of Windsor has some ideal training roads on its doorstep.
Attractions	Windsor Great Park, Windsor town and Castle, Eton and the Thames.
Refreshments	Untold teashops in Windsor and Eton, where you can practice your French, German and Spanish. The Saville Gardens Restaurant in the Great Park. The Fox and Castle - Old Windsor.

Windsor is dominated by its huge Castle and the town centre is pinched between its curving wall and a bend in the Thames. The Guildhall on the High Street (1) was begun in 1686 and completed by Christopher Wren. It is said that Wren added the central line of pillars only at the insistence of the town's doubting burghers, who were afraid the outer ranks would be insufficient to support the Guild Chamber above. To show his contempt for their anxiety, Wren had the pillars built too short to touch the floor and the gap remains.

With your back to the Castle turn right down the High Street, which bends left around the Curfew Tower and becomes Thames Street. Follow the one-way system and turn left by the Sun pub to the Eton/Windsor Bridge which is closed to all but pedestrian traffic.

The bridge, a rare example of early cast-iron work, was opened in 1824. Eton High Street is narrow and atmospheric and runs from the bridge to the Eton College. Look out for the fifteenth century timber cockpit. An old enamel sign-post 'Maidenhead 6' recalls a less distant era. The College was set up five and a half centuries ago for the education of 70 poor scholars, these days outnumbered by 1200 rich ones.

At the end of the High Street (2) (0.5 miles) within the College turn right onto Windsor Road and pass the Wall where the Eton Wall Game is played, with one goal scored every thirty years. Cross the water-meadows and sports grounds and turn right into Pococks Lane for Datchet. Turn right onto the B376 signed for Wraysbury and Staines and right over the railway level-crossing when you reach Datchet High Street (3) (2 miles). Turn left when you reach the riverside. On your right is Datchet Meads where Shakespeare hid Falstaff in the washing.

Cross Albert Bridge and go straight on at the roundabout into Straight Road, Old Windsor. Turn right at the Wheatsheaf pub into St Lukes Road (4) (4.5 miles). When this road forks, take the right leg, Crimp Hill. Crimp Hill is the only significant climb on the route. In general, stopping at the top rather than the bottom of hills is recommended, but it is worth making an exception for The Fox and Castle, an old ale house set back from the road a few yards down the left fork Burfield Road. It has a garden with a children's playground where bikes can be parked in relative safety. The fact that it is a little out of the way means the food and service are better than in the tourist traps on the other side of the route. This road also leads in about a mile to the historic riverside area of Runnymede.

Crimp Hill lasts for more than a mile but has only one steep section. Turn right at the top onto Bishopsgate Road and enter Windsor Great Park through the white wooden gates (5) (6 miles). Keep right in front of the pink Bishops Gate House and ride to the gates. Reach up to push a button set at a convenient height for horse riders and the gates open noiselessly to give access to the Deer Park. The mechanised gates are rather spooky, like entering the lair of a James Bond super-villain.

The roadway is smooth and unmarked. Motor vehicles are restricted and few pedestrians venture far from the gates. You are soon alone. Looking north you see the Castle, three miles away but enormous. It looks like a painted backdrop. If the wind is in the east a steady procession of Heathrow-bound jets hang in the sky. Beyond the Castle is the level sprawl of the western suburbs, but closer is only meticulously maintained parkland with stands of ancient oak. The combination of immaculate surroundings and sudden absence of traffic or crowds gives the feeling of riding across a film set. Rounding a corner to see the oversized equestrian statue of George III,

the 'Copper Horse', above you heightens the sense of weirdness.

Cycling is not permitted on the Long Walk which extends dead straight north to the Castle. Keep left after the second gate (this one opens on its own) (6) (7.5 miles). The occasional cars in the park tend to be swift and silent, so don't let the fairy-tale surroundings send you to sleep completely. Go straight on at the crossroads which marks the centre of this figure-of-eight route.

Duke's Lane brings you to Ascot Gate (7) (9.5 miles). Descend through the exotic mix of trees and shrubs to merge with the B383. At the bottom of the hill, turn left into Mill Lane which follows a small water course to reach the ornamental lakes of Virginia Water. Built by the Sandby brothers on the orders of William Duke of Cumberland who the Scots named 'Billy the Butcher' for his ethnic cleansing after the Battle of Culloden. Turn left into Blacknest Gate (8) (11 miles). Over another arm of Virginia Water and climbing, on your right a footpath leads to Valley Gardens, a compendious collection of Rhododendrons.

The road levels onto the manicured expanse of Smith's Lawn, where polo and other equestrian events are staged.

Even if there are no sports taking place it is common to see strings of magnificent ponies being exercised in the park. If you think some bikes are expensive, don't even consider developing an interest in polo. On your left is another giant statue. This one to Albert the Prince Consort. In the early years of the nineteenth century the decadent monarchy was unpopular and revolution in France a living memory. By redefining the perception of the monarch as servant of state and people, Albert ensured the institution survived almost to the end of the twentieth century. He is the person most responsible for the odd atmosphere of the park. The contradiction between its scale and condition, which indicate fabulous private wealth, and its semi-dedication to the quiet pleasure of the public, show the desire of the monarchy to persist. A right turn at the top of Smith's Lawn takes you on a detour to the restaurant at Saville's Gardens.

At Cumberland Lodge (9) (13 miles) where two paths branch left, take the second past five stone balls. Bear right at the Chaplains Lodge downhill and keep right at the next fork. Repass the cross roads. Pass the Village, a model estate built in the late Forties for Park employees, with its green, and fake, bow-fronted Post office, a parody of English rural harmony. Turn right after the Village (10) (14.5 miles) and continue to the Park exit at Rangers Lodge. Turn right onto the A332. This road is nicely unimproved but brings you back to the hustling reality of south east England. Follow it to the large roundabout (11) (16.5 miles) and take the second exit into King's Road which continues into Sheet Street. At the end of this, a left turn leads into the High street which leads to the Guildhall (1) (17 miles).

BETWEEN MAIDENHEAD & BRACKNELL

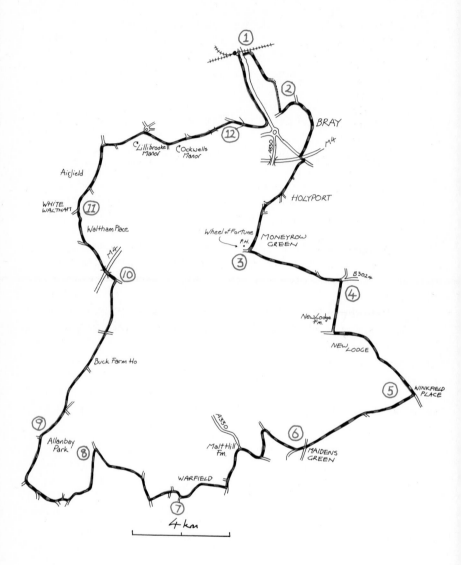

Lillibrooke Manor

Cockwells Manor

Airfield

WHITE WALTHAM

Waltham Place

M4

Buck Farm Ho

Allanbay Park

BRAY

M4

HOLYPORT

Wheel of Fortune P.H.

MONEYROW GREEN

A330

B3024

New Lodge Fm.

NEW LODGE

WINKFIELD PLACE

A330

Malt Hill Fm.

WARFIELD

MAIDENS GREEN

4 km

BETWEEN MAIDENHEAD & BRACKNELL

Map	OS LR 175 Reading and Windsor.
Start	Maidenhead BR Station, trains from Paddington. Parking in the multi-storey in Stafferton Way.
Finish	Maidenhead BR Station.
Distance	21 miles.
Route	An easy circuit of the country between Maidenhead, Windsor and Bracknell with very little climbing.
Attractions	Brunel's bridge and Boulter's Lock in Maidenhead, quiet lanes and the villages of Bray, Warfield, Binfield and White Waltham.
Refreshments	Although it is about two miles from the route, the Café on the Thames at Boulters Lock is recommended.

Maidenhead owes its existence to two routes. In the days of the coach, it was an important stage town on the Bath Road. At its height, 90 coaches a day would rattle down its narrow High Street. Later the railway made it a glamorous resort - the 'jewel of the Thames' - where playboys and debutantes came to dine and flaunt their wealth on the river.

Turn right out of Maidenhead Station (1) and right again to pass under the tracks on the A308 to the roundabout. Take the first exit into Stafferton Way. Just before this industrial cul-de-sac bridges a stream, turn right onto the unmarked black-top track which runs between the stream and allotments. Be prepared to give way to pedestrians. The shallow steps at Green Lane can be ridden with a little care. Turn right and carry on down the overhung path. Bear right then left to emerge on Hibbert Road (2) (1 mile). Turn left to reach the village of Bray by bike or right and left into The Causeway to follow a pleasantly overgrown footpath to the same destination. If you want to detour north turn left. Otherwise turn right.

Going north gives a chance to admire the widest flattest brick-built arch in the world. Follow the B3028 north and turn right just before it goes under the railway to reach the river. This bridge, 128 feet wide and only 24 feet high, was built in 1839 by Isambard Kingdom Brunel to carry the Great Western Railway to Bath and Bristol, and features in Turner's painting 'Rain, Steam and Speed'. If you carry on even further along the B3028 to meet the A4 London Road and then turn right to the river, the elegant road bridge is a good spot to further admire Brunel's wonder. From here you can follow the Thames Path North to Boulter's Lock, where there are pleasant public gardens on Ray Mill Island - the old flour mill has been converted into a hotel. Retrace your route to reach Bray village.

Go through the village and cross the A308 by going left then right under the M4 into Holyport Road. At Holyport keep left around the village green and carry on through the ribbon development to Moneyrow Green. Turn left at the Wheel of Fortune pub (3) (4 miles) onto the B3024 for Fifield. The fine elms along this road died from Dutch elm disease in 1980, but the hedgerows survive. Owls may be seen at dusk and in the early morning.

Turn right in Fifield (4) (5 miles), signposted Winkfield and Ascot. Climb the road to New Lodge Farm, pausing to look back over the Thames Valley to Ashley Hill. A mile past New Lodge turn right into Winkfield

Lane (5) (7.5 miles), signed for Maidens Green. Notice the old houses along this road, like 'The Pump Room', a listed building with central entry and huge oak door.

At Maidens Green (6) (9 miles) go over the crossroads and 100m further after Tory Hall Farm and Abbey Farm, turn right into Bishops Lane. Keep left until you reach the A330. Turn right and after about 400m, left signposted for Warfield. At Malt Hill, Bracknell appears on the skyline but we stay well outside the town boundary.

Turn right down Church Lane signposted Warfield Church, and take the next unsigned road on the right (7) (11 miles) and follow it to a T junction on the A 3095. Turn right and follow the A road for only about 400m then turn left into an unsigned road. From this road you can take the first left which is a muddy bridleway or the second which is a metalled lane (8) (12.5 miles).

If you choose the bridleway turn right at the T junction into Cabbage Hill Lane and then right just over the bridge, and left just before another bridge to pass the cemetery. If you take the clean route you will come to the former ford from the otherside to cross the low level bridge - the higher foot bridge is for use in times of flood, and turn right past the cemetery. Join the B3018 and turn right, take this road past Binfield Church.

This area has no stone but in some places its beds of sand and pebbles have hardened naturally to form boulders of a conglomerate rock 'Berkshire Sarsens'. All Saints Church in Binfield incorporates blocks of this tough sandstone, as does the Church at White Waltham.

At Allanbay Park (9) (14.5 miles) turn right off the B3018, following the signs for Paley Street, White Waltham and Maidenhead. This road crosses the stream at Bucks Farm, built in 1829. Further on, the water's straight course, together with the trees on its bank suggest it has been diverted to drain the land. This is confirmed by the map which names it 'The Cut'. The work must have been long ago for the watercourse now blends well with its surroundings.

On arrival at the T junction on the B3024 (10) (17 miles) turn left over the M4, then right signposted Woodlands Park, Cox Green. Turn right at the T junction past White Waltham Church (11) (18 miles). On your right is White Waltham Airfield home of the West London Aero Club. At Woodlands Park turn right at the mini-roundabout. Turn right onto Ockwells Road just before the next roundabout.

Keep straight on at the small triangular green past the cul-de-sac sign and the Farriers Arms restaurant. Ockwells Road has been cut by the 404M, which must be crossed on a ramped concrete bridleway bridge (12) (20 miles). On the other side of the bridge fork left, then turn right onto Manor Lane, then left at the T junction on Harvest Hill Road. A right turn at a final T junction begins a descent into town which brings you to the back entrance of the railway station (1) (21 miles).

BURNHAM BEECHES -
LIFE BEYOND SLOUGH

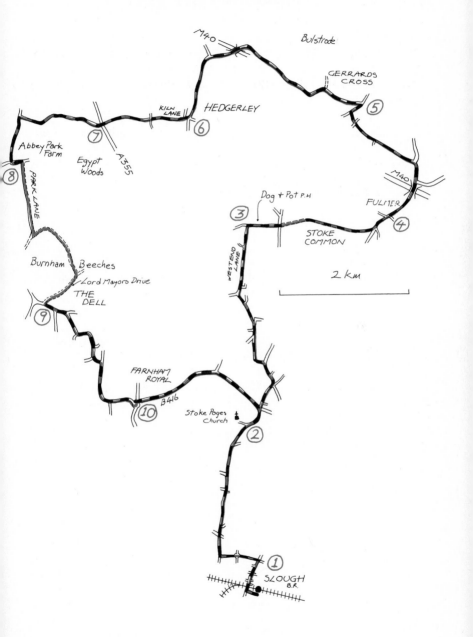

BURNHAM BEECHES -
LIFE BEYOND SLOUGH

Map	OS LR 175 Reading and Windsor covers all the route except a short and simple section after Fulmer which is on the LR 176 West London area.
Start	Slough Station. Trains from Paddington. Car park on Lord Mayors Drive at the eastern side of Burnham Beeches.
Finish	Slough Station.
Distance	19 miles with plenty of hills.
Route	North through Stoke Poges to the edge of Gerrards Cross, west via the hidden village of Hedgerley to return to Slough through Burnham Beeches.
Attractions	Stoke Poges Church and Common, Fulmer, Hedgerley, Burnham Beeches.
Refreshments	Pub in Fulmer and two pubs in Hedgerley. Seven Day Chippy (and Indian Sweets) in Stoke Poges Lane - Slough. The Dell tea hut in Burnham Beeches.

At Slough station (1) turn right then right again over the railway on Stoke Road. Turn left into Belgrave Road and follow it over the mini-roundabout to come to Stoke Poges Lane opposite the combined Indian sweets and chipshop, open seven days a week. Turn right and go straight on at the traffic lights over the Berkshire/Buckinghamshire border and shrug off the last of Slough.

The road becomes Church Lane and on the left is Stoke Poges Church (2) (1.5 miles). The Church is famous as the setting for Thomas Gray's 'Elegy written in a Country Churchyard' published in 1750. There is a monument to Gray in a field beside the church. It was erected after his death by John Penn, grandson of the founder of Pennsylvania. In those days Slough was a hamlet on the Bath Road, the southern limit of the Parish of Stoke Poges. It was Slough's rapid growth in the inter-war period that prompted Betjeman's plea 'come friendly bombs and fall on Slough it isn't fit for humans now'. Betjeman was a prime mover of the 1977 campaign to have Gray's monument restored and is the only Poet Laureate to mention the Sturmey-Archer gear in his work.

At the crossroads go straight on to Church Lane and at the T junction turn left into the B416 signposted Stoke Poges and Gerrards Cross. Take the first left into Rogers Lane. Turn right at the T junction into a continuation of Rogers Lane and left at the Dog and Pot pub into Duffield Lane. The road is sheltered from both sides by hedges reinforced with fine mature trees. The gradient is shallow and even and the road has a smooth surface. It is superb for cycling. The lane leaves the houses behind and opens out onto fine countryside. If you feel a poem coming on this is as good a place as any to put pen to paper.

The lane reaches a T junction (3) (4 miles). Turn right onto Templewood Lane. Cross the B416 into Stoke Common Road. This road runs nicely down among the trees of the Common. At the end turn left and continue down into Fulmer (4) (5 miles) which with its newly painted houses, its cute Post Office complete with enamel advertisements and gleaming vintage postbox looks ready to enter a best kept village contest. Climb out of Fulmer over the rumble of the M40, and on entering the fringes of Gerrards Cross turn left into Fulmer Drive.

At first the large detached houses are pure stockbroker belt, higher up they are built so close together that their detachment is no more than symbolic. At the T junction turn right onto the B416 and left (5) (6.5 miles) onto Hedgerley Lane. The lane goes down steeply around the high brick perimeter wall of Bullstrode Park then climbs again to run alongside then cross the M40 before dropping into Hedgerley (6) (9 miles). This village may outdo Fulmer in the picturesque stakes. It has a tiny old school, now a dwelling, and a duck pond. Turn right into Kiln Lane by the Brick Mould pub. Hedgerley was famous for its bricks in the 17th and 18th centuries thanks to the sandy loam in the area.

When the lane turns right into Andrew Hill Lane keep straight ahead on the bridleway. This sandy track remains unsurfaced for 500 yards - within living memory all country lanes were like this - then climbs through Penlands Farm yard to join a metalled drive. Cross the A355 (7) (10 miles) into Harehatch lane. At the T junction turn left and roll down past Abbey Park Farm (8) (11.5 miles) to Burnham Beeches.

This remarkably wild stretch of ancient countryside is the highlight of the ride and well worth taking time to explore. You can afford to get lost because the owners of the land - The Corporation of London have put up frequent signboards with maps and location. Two hundred years ago this was heathland common grazed by free-ranging cattle, pigs and goats. The beech trees were pollarded - cropped systematically for firewood and winter fodder. The absence of grazing in the twentieth century has led to the growth of dense secondary woodland among the ancient trees.

At the second green signboard take a sharp left into Morton Drive. Carry on to Hardicanute's Moat where the woods contain the remains of a mediaeval homestead. Keep right into Halse Drive which descends into a dell before climbing steeply to Victory Cross. Turn right into Lord Mayor's Drive and carry on to emerge from the Beeches by The Dell open-air cafe (9) (13.5 miles).

Turn left then second right. At the T junction turn left into East Burnham Lane. Keep left at East Burnham Park and at the T junction turn right. Turn left into Crown lane to bring you to Farnham Royal (10) (15 miles). Turn left then right at the two small roundabouts to take the B416 back to Stoke Poges where, by turning right into Church Lane you can return to much maligned Slough (1) (19 miles).

AMONG THE THREE HUNDREDS

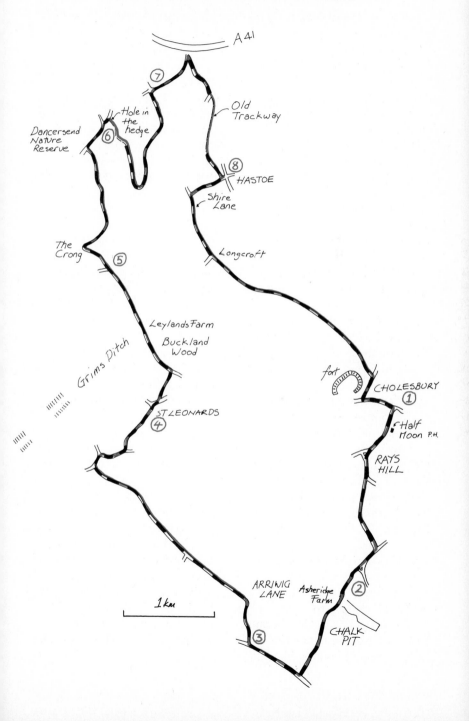

A 41

⑦

Old Trackway

Hole in the hedge

Dancersend Nature Reserve

⑥

⑧ HASTOE

Shire Lane

The Crong

⑤

Longcroft

Leylands Farm

Buckland Wood

Grims Ditch

ST LEONARDS

④

fort

CHOLESBURY
①

Half Moon P.H.

RAYS HILL

1 km

ARRIWIG LANE

Asheridge Farm

②

③

CHALK PIT

AMONG THE THREE HUNDREDS

Map	OS LR 165 Aylesbury and Leighton Buzzard
Start	Cholesbury village. Railway Stations Tring (from Euston), Chesham, Great Missenden or Wendover (from Marylebone) - all about 3 or 4 miles away. BR Information Tring 071 387 7070. Other stations 071 262 6767. By road via Rickmansworth, Chess valley and Chesham.
Finish	Same as Start.
Distance	12 miles.
Route	Through quiet lanes with some short steep climbs and short sections on unmade roads.
Attractions	Cholesbury village, St. Leonards, Grim's Ditch.
Refreshments	Cholesbury Village.

This little excursion in the Chilterns incorporates several scenes of gentle chalk and clay valleys and ridges with many traditional flint cottages. It extends up to the escarpment which marks the northern limit of the Chilterns, where on a clear day, the views into the Midlands across the Vale of Aylesbury offer a contrast to the quiet intimacy of the Range's wooded hollows. You will encounter few cars and fewer tourists.

Historically the Chiltern Hills were known as a hiding place for bands of brigands and outlaws, because the whole area was so heavily forested. It is claimed that, right into the seventeenth century, Celtic tribes (or at least their direct descendants) lived in these valleys above Chesham.

Place names along the route indicate the density of the forest. Dancersend and Painesend, for example, indicate that one could penetrate no further. Where you find the suffix 'ridge' as in Chartridge or Hawridge, it marks settlements that developed on the ridges where passage was easier. These ridges were settled first and the roads running along them have tended to develop into main routes. Most of the routes crossing the valleys remain as simple trackways (their legal status may be footpath, bridleway, byway or country road).

The starting point is Cholesbury village (1). Leave the village down Ray's Hill, which leaves the main road through the village near the Windmill. The road dips and rises sharply. This is a feature of the Chilterns and these small steep-sided valleys are known as 'chines' by the locals. At the top, turn left by the pond and when the road bears left, take the lesser lane straight ahead; when the lane bears left, go ahead along the drive signed Ashridge Farm (2) (1 mile).

Follow the bridleway around the farm buildings. Within the woods on the left, just where the track begins its dip into the chine, there is and old, overgrown, chalk pit, a good place for a refreshment stop or to do some flower hunting. Continue along the track; it is mostly well surfaced with flint, but can be muddy in patches after wet weather, especially in the loamy bottom of the chine. The track climbs again and you reach Chartridge, where you turn right, and then take the next right, signed Arriwig Lane (3) (2 miles).

This lane is unremarkable except for its curious name, but soon after dipping down another chine, you climb onto a ridge crossing open farmland where, on a clear day, there are good views across the undulating and wooded landscape. At the end of the lane turn right and right again at the bottom and then climb to St. Leonards (4) (5 miles).

At the wooden church at St. Leonards, turn right and take the next left, turning left again at the bottom. There is now a very gradual climb past Leylands Farm, where you may discern the course of Grim's Ditch, which crosses our lane at this point. This pre-historic earth bank and ditch runs for many miles the whole length of the Chilterns. Its origins and purpose are unknown, and its presence is more distinct in other places. Soon the lane dives down the scarp slope (5) (6 miles).

Halfway down, the lane turns sharp right at a bend called The Crong. Continue down then up to Spencersgreen and up and down to Ebbs Pit, another overgrown chalk pit on a sharp right hander. Opposite this is a small track leading to Dancersend Nature Reserve, run by BBONT (the Buckinghamshire, Berkshire and Oxfordshire Nature Trust) and only open to the public occasionally.

Continue uphill to Dancersend, where through a gateway on the right, you can look across undulating farmland to the ridge beyond.

Where the lane forks, keep straight on into Duckmore Lane and almost immediately find a hole in the hedge on the right (6) (7.5 miles). This is an old country road which has become over-grown through disuse. It can get muddy and the surface is broken by horse traffic but because it is going gently downhill it can be ridden. After 500 m it steepens and requires some care before emerging onto a remote narrow lane which winds its way along the valley bottom through Painesend and Terrier's End, to rejoin Duckmore Lane (7) (8 miles).

Turn right and continue. Just before going under the A41 Tring Bypass Motorway turn sharp right. This lane climbs past Upper West Leith Farm and turns into an old country trackway. This is a long steep climb which makes a testing challenge or a pleasant walk depending on your fitness or inclination. The lower section is cut into the chalk with dense undergrowth for shade and shelter. Higher the path is more open among mature beech trees, with patches of sky and views north towards Buckingham. At the top, after the track merges with the drive of a house, turn right and join Shire Lane (8) (10 miles), so-named because it is the border between Hertfordshire and Buckinghamshire. This long, gradual descent, which crosses

Grim's Ditch again at Longcroft, makes a very pleasant end to the trip and brings you right back to Cholesbury (1) (12 miles).

If this has been a morning ride, you should have just enough time for a late lunch at the Half Moon Pub. Afterwards you can explore the ironage earthwork, with a church within. There is cricket on the village green on summer Sundays.

BEYOND THE MIGHTY CHILTERNS

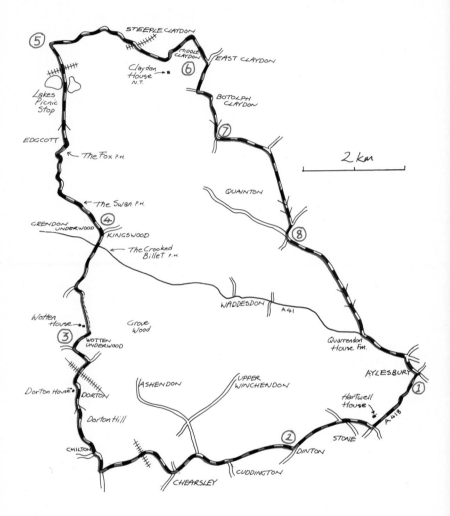

BEYOND THE MIGHTY CHILTERNS

Map	OS LR 165 Aylesbury and Leighton Buzzard.
Start	Aylesbury Station Tel: 0494 441561. Chiltern Turbos from Marylebone have limited space for cycles and include rush hour restrictions. On Sundays you can take the tube to Amersham and change to BR for Aylesbury.
Finish	Aylesbury Station. Car Parking at Station and around the town centre.
Distance	37 miles including 1 mile of well-made but sometimes overgrown off-road.
Route	A loop running North from Aylesbury over a few low hills and across shallow river valleys.
Attractions	The Villages of Cuddington and Chearsley along the River Thame. Wotton House and Claydon House. Calvert Brick Works and Clay Pits Nature Reserve.
Refreshments	Annie Bailey's - Cuddington, The Crooked Billet. - Kingswood, The Swan - Grendon Underwood, The Fox - Edgcott, Tea Rooms - Claydon House.

Turn left outside the Station (1) and follow the road past the supermarket. Turn left at the roundabout then left again onto the A418 Oxford Road. This road crosses the railway then runs level and fairly straight. The stone wall of the grounds of Hartwell House on the right announces the village of Hartwell. The Jacobean mansion was the residence of Louis the XVIII in the Napoleonic period. Now it is a hotel and restaurant. Follow the main road to the right past the milestone outside the Bugle Horn Pub.

Next comes the village of Stone where a late Norman church has a carved font. All along this road you can view the wooded wave of the Chiltern escarpment to your left. Beyond Stone turn right on the road signposted 'Cuddington, Chearsley, Long Crendon (2) (4.5 miles). Cuddington is a pretty village of stone and thatch. A diversion down the roads on the right will reveal more old buildings clustered round the Church and Annie Bailey's Eating House if you have you've remembered to pack your credit card. On down to cross the River Tame running indecisively westward into Oxfordshire where it turns south to feed the Thames.

Climb into Chearsley. If you liked Cuddington explore the lanes down to the left of the Village green. The terrace of cottages in School Lane used to house Lace Makers and the area around Watts Green was the commercial district. The nail-maker's shed still stands in the garden of 'Needlemakers' cottage. The house opposite used to have a matching cobbler's shop. Exit from the top of the Village on the road signposted Chilton and Dorton.

The road descends to pass under the railway. Once through the bridge the road climbs to turn right at the T junction to reach Chilton. An alternative is to walk the footpath which leaves the road on the right at the foot of the hill and cuts the corner to rejoin the route in the village. The stretch of road after Chilton is a fine rolling descent lined with trees but exposed. The distant, disused chimneys of the London Brick Company mark the northern most part of the route. On your left is the hill top village of Brill, used as a demanding finish for local road-races so if it's a Sunday and a pack of brilliantly clad masochists come whizzing past with numbers on their backs, you will know why.

Continue through Dorton which was unsuccessfully promoted as a Spar in the early 19th Century. Cross the railway (3) (12 miles) and turn left signposted Brill, Ludgershall, Bicester and Wotton.

At the sign 'Wotton Only' turn right. Wotton Church contains an impressive array of tombs of the Grenville Family. Richard Grenville built Wotton House in 1704. Pass the main entrance to the house and go through the wooden kissing gate at the footpath sign to the left. This path is surfaced with concrete slab. In Summer it can be overgrown with nettles making for a tricky passage in shorts. The path passes in front of the House. It was restored in 1820 by John Soane after being gutted by fire. Cross the open land, with newly planted trees, and continues through the garden of a humbler dwelling. It then joins a dirt road. At the junction with the metalled road turn right.

At Kingswood we cross the A41 (4) (15.5 miles) running on the course of Akeman Street, a Roman Road. Don't turn left for Bicester and Birmingham or right for Aylesbury and London but carry straight on past the wayside Chapel. Turn left for Grendon Underwood and right at the bottom of its long main street by the church. Like many settlements on old coach routes Grendon once had a muddy reputation. 'Grendon Underwood the dirtiest town that ever stood'. The problems caused by unpaved tracks, heavy clay soil, rain and horses hooves are not new. Local legend claims Shakespeare stayed at the Ship Inn, now known as Shakespeare House. Which given the proximity of the Stratford-London Road is plausible. The oak framed tudor brick building stands near to the church.

The Shakespeare story may be meant to boost the tourist trade but at the moment a large number of Grendon Underwood's visitors are not voluntary. The road skirts the big open prison and continues through Edgcott. Turn left onto the Buckingham road. Out of Edgcott the road crosses a low hill. The land beyond it is drained by North flowing rivers which join the Great Ouse at Buckingham. We now pass the ranks of the brick works chimneys at the Calvert Works. Construction of the factory began in 1898 and bricks were produced from 1900. At its peak in the period of reconstruction after the Second World War the works employed more than 1,000 workers. Over the crossroads are two flooded clay-pits the one on the left is a private boat club but the other is a nature reserve. Through the wooden gate in the lay-by a concrete path leads down to a wooden hide. Approach it quietly so as not to disturb any bird-watchers inside.

Cross the single track railway (5) (20.5 miles) and turn right to Steeple Claydon, a village which owes its size and prosperity to the Brick Works, and its name to the sticky soil which was baked there. The brick workers settled here because this was the nearest village with piped water and a sewage system. On through Middle Claydon (6) (24.5 miles) dominated by Claydon House the home of the Verney family since 1543. The house is closed for renovation at the time of writing but has a good Tea Shop when open. In the Church of All Saints you can see the gauntlet of Sir Edmund Verney, the King's Standard Bearer killed at the Battle of Edge Hill. His hand, clutching the flag pole, so the story goes, was all they found of his body.

Turn right at the T junction of Sandhill and right again in East Claydon. The three Claydons plus the hamlet of Botolph Claydon grew up originally to house the Claydon Estate workers. Through Botolph Claydon turn left then right,

following the signs for Quainton. Turn Left (7) (28 miles) along the gated road signed North Marston. This road, unfenced along the foot of bleak north facing sheep pasture on Quainton Hill has the feel of the North Country. At the farm buildings turn right onto another Roman Road. At the end of this road (8) (31 miles) turn right and left at the cross.

On the right is the impressive wooded hill top of Waddesdon Manor on Akeman Street. Ahead through a forest of pylons is Aylesbury. Turn left onto the A41. The single tower block on the skyline marks the town centre and your distance to the finish. Through the suburbs you are crossing the site of the Civil War Battle of Aylesbury. On reaching the ring road you can either turn right to get straight back to the station (9) (37 miles) or go on to explore the motor-traffic free town centre.

RIDE CONTRIBUTORS

1. LONDON'S PARKS & REGENTS CANAL — Patrick Field
2. THE WEST END TO DOCKLANDS — Patrick Field
3. THE TOURIST'S TRACK — Peter Jacobson
4. THE LEA & THE MIMRAM — Barrie Wood - CTC St. Albans & Hatfield
5. THE RODING & THE CAM — Patrick Field
6. ESSEX IS NOT FLAT — Patrick Field
7. THE DARENT TO DICKENS' ROCHESTER — Patrick Field
8. THE PILGRIMS WAY — Tim Cox - CTC
9. GREENSAND RIDGE WEST — Tim Cox - CTC
10. GREENSAND RIDGE EAST — Tim Cox - CTC
11. DOWN TO RYE & ROMNEY MARSH — Charles Tallack
12. EDEN VALE & HIGH ROCKS — Tim Cox - CTC
13. ASHDOWN & THE BLUEBELL RAILWAY — Michael Collins
14. DOWNSLINK SOUTH — Michael Collins
15. ARUNDEL & THE DOWNS — Tim Cox - CTC
16. DOWNSLINK NORTH — Dave Frohock
17. LEITH HILL & THE SURREY WEALD — Tim Cox - CTC
18. MOLE VALLEY & BOX HILL — Clive Oxx - CTC SW London
19. THE THAMES TOWPATH — Clive Oxx - CTC SW London
20. WINDSOR & VIRGINIA WATER — Richard Mackrory - CTC Slough
21. MAIDENHEAD & BRACKNELL — Raymond Fox - CTC Windsor
22. BURNHAM BEECHES — Richard Mackrory - CTC Slough
23. AMONG THE THREE HUNDREDS — Geoff Apps
24. BEYOND THE MIGHTY CHILTERNS — David Matthews - CTC Aylesbury

ORGANISATION ADDRESSES

ALARM UK
c/o Lambeth Public Transport Group
13 Stockwell Road, London SW9.
071 737 6641

BRITISH CYCLING FEDERATION (BCF)
36 Rockingham Road, Kettering,
Northants, NN16 8HG.
0536 412211

BIKE 1
PO Box 105, Fleet, Hampshire, GU1 38YR.
Tel: 0252 624022   Fax: 0252 624942

BIKE EVENTS
PO Box 75, Bath, Avon, BA1 1BX.
0225 480130

BRITISH MOUNTAIN BIKE FEDERATION (BMBF)
Same as BCF.

CYCLING TUTORIALS
Moto Sport, Smithbrook Kilns, Cranleigh, Surrey.
0483 278282

CYCLISTS' TOURING CLUB (CTC)
Cotterell House, 69 Meadrow, Godalming,
Surrey, GU7 3HS. 0483 417217

ENVIRONMENTAL TRANSPORT ASSOCIATION
(ETA) The Old Post House, Heath Road, Weybridge, KT13 8RS.

LONDON CYCLING CAMPAIGN (LCC)
3 Stamford Street, London, SE1 9NT. 071 928 7220

LONDON SCHOOL OF CYCLING
147 Amhurst Road, London, E8 2AW. 071 249 3779

RECLAIM THE STREETS ACTION NETWORK
PO Box 1593, London, SW9 8LT. 071 737 0100

TANDEM CLUB
Membership Secretary, 41 Royston Avenue,
Southend-on-Sea, SS2 5JY.

TRANSPORT USERS CONSULTATIVE COMMITTEE - LONDON AREA
5th Floor, Golden House, Duncannon Street,
London, WC2N 4JF.

SUSTRANS
35 King Street, Bristol, Avon, BS1 4DZ.
0272 268893
Sustrans is a charity which builds cycle paths and
other facilities for cyclists.